A-Z
Street Atlas of
CARDI...

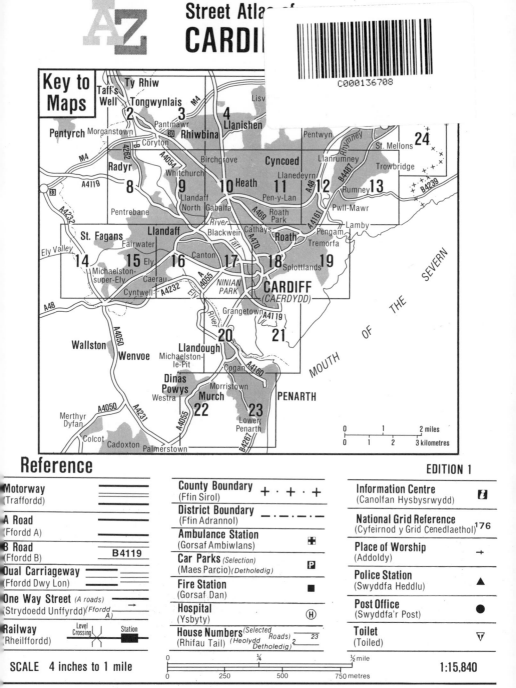

Key to Maps

Taff's Well, Ty Rhiw, Tongwynlais, Lisv..., Pentyrch, Morganstown, Pantmawr, Rhiwbina, Llanishen, Coryton, Pentwyn, Rhymney, St. Mellons, 24, Birchgrove, Cyncoed, Llanrumney, Trowbridge, Radyr, Whitchurch, Heath, Llanedeyrn, Rumney, 13, Llandaff North, Gabalfa, Pen-y-Lan, Pwll-Mawr, Pentrebane, River, Roath Park, Lamby, St. Fagans, Llandaff, Blackwein, Cathays, Roath, Pengam, Tremorfa, Fairwater, Canton, Splottlands, 19, Michaelston-super-Ely, Caerau, Cyntwell, NINIAN PARK, CARDIFF (CAERDYDD), Grangetown, Wallston, Wenvoe, Llandough, Michaelston-le-Pit, Cogan, Dinas Powys, Morristown, PENARTH, Westra, Murch, Merthyr Dyfan, Lower Penarth, Colcot, Cadoxton, Palmerstown

0 ... 1 ... 2 miles
0 ... 1 ... 2 ... 3 kilometres

Reference

EDITION 1

Motorway (Trafford)	
A Road (Ffordd A)	
B Road (Ffordd B)	B4119
Dual Carriageway (Ffordd Dwy Lôn)	
One Way Street (A roads) (Strydoedd Unffyrdd)(Ffordd A)	→
Railway (Rheilffordd)	Level Crossing / Station

County Boundary (Ffin Sirol)	+ · + · +
District Boundary (Ffin Adrannol)	— · — · —
Ambulance Station (Gorsaf Ambiwlans)	✚
Car Parks (Selection) (Maes Parcio)(Detholedig)	P
Fire Station (Gorsaf Dân)	■
Hospital (Ysbyty)	Ⓗ
House Numbers (Selected Roads) (Rhifau Tail) (Heolydd Detholedig)	23 / 2

Information Centre (Canolfan Hysbysrwydd)	ℹ
National Grid Reference (Cyfeirnod y Grid Cenedlaethol)	176
Place of Worship (Addoldy)	✝
Police Station (Swyddfa Heddlu)	▲
Post Office (Swyddfa'r Post)	●
Toilet (Toiled)	▽

SCALE 4 inches to 1 mile

0 ... ¼ ... ½ mile
0 ... 250 ... 500 ... 750 metres

1:15,840

Geographers' A-Z Map Company Limited

Head Office: Vestry Road, Sevenoaks, Kent, TN14 5EP. Telephone 0732 451152
Showrooms: 44 Gray's Inn Road, Holborn, London, WC1X 8LR. Telephone 01 242 9246

ISBN 0 85039 203 9

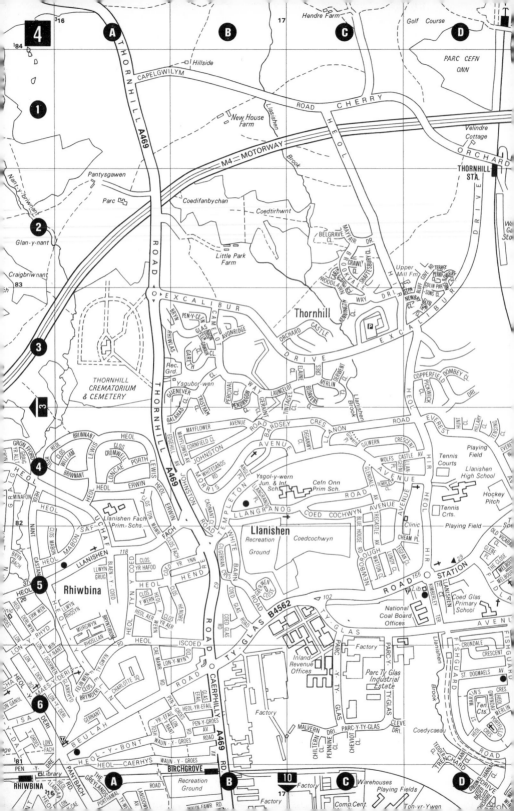

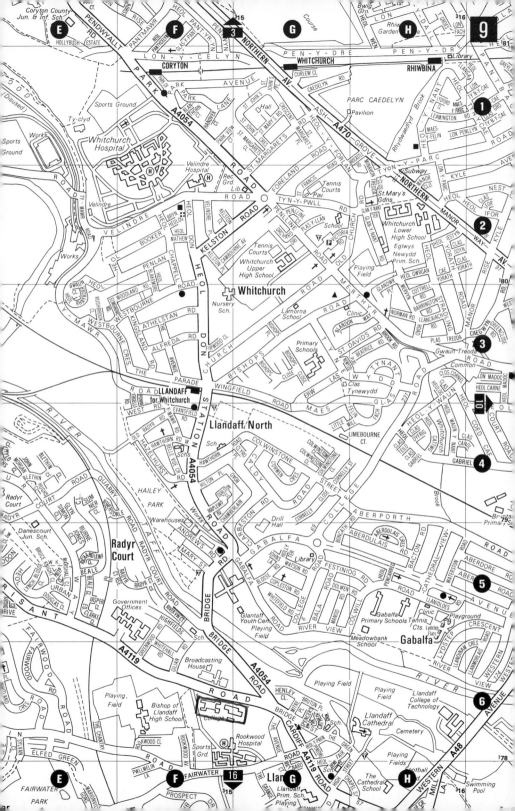

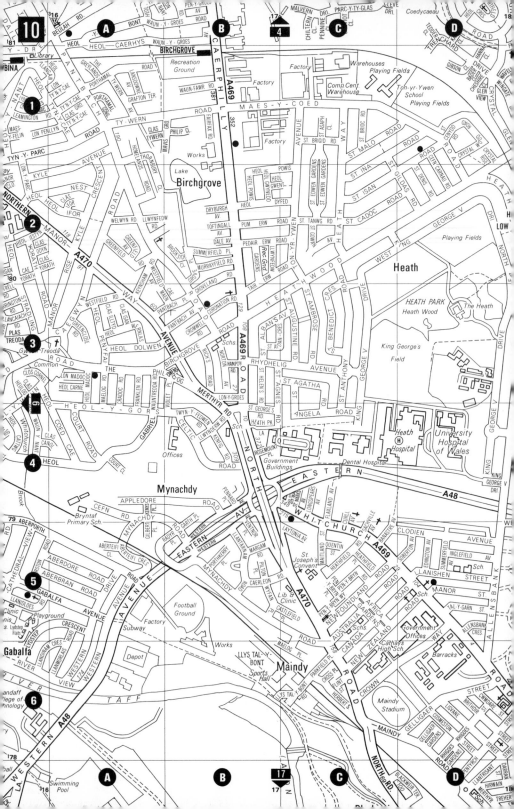

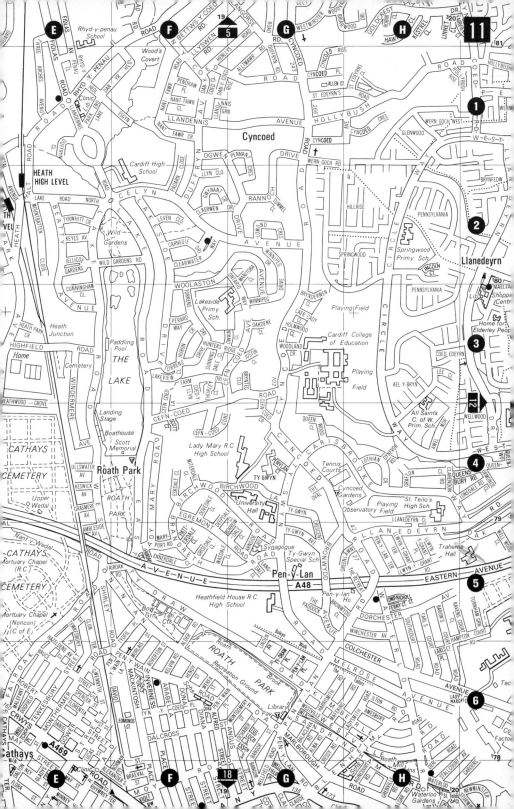

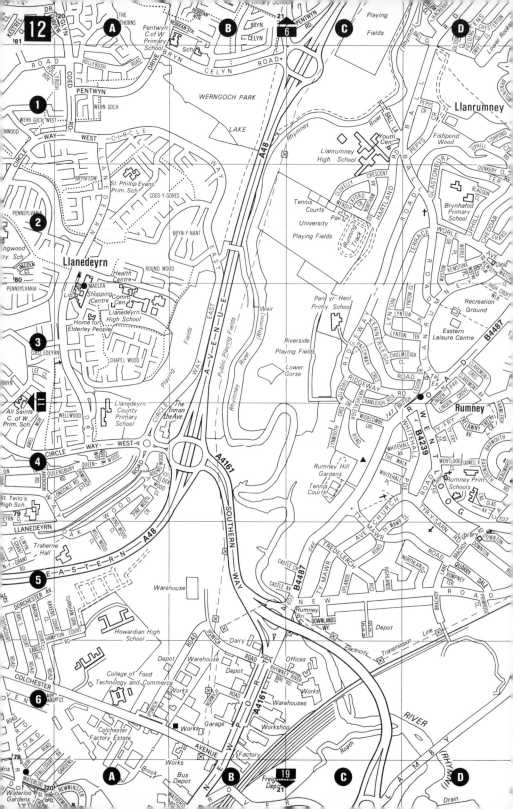

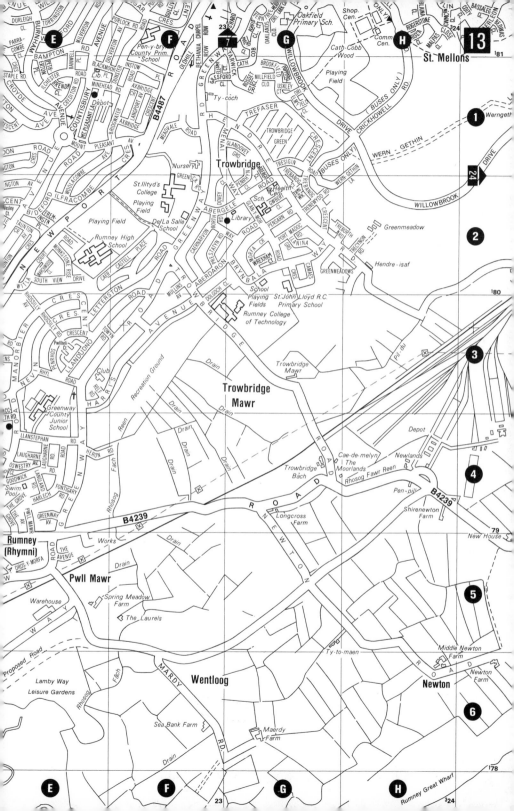

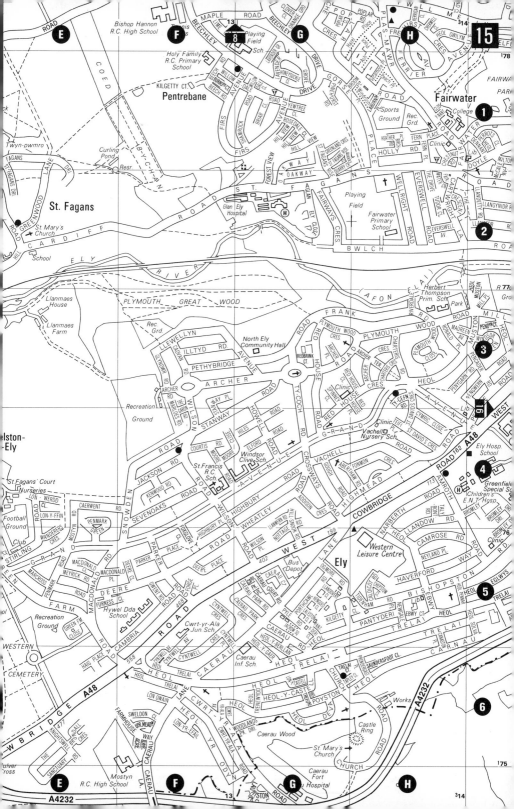

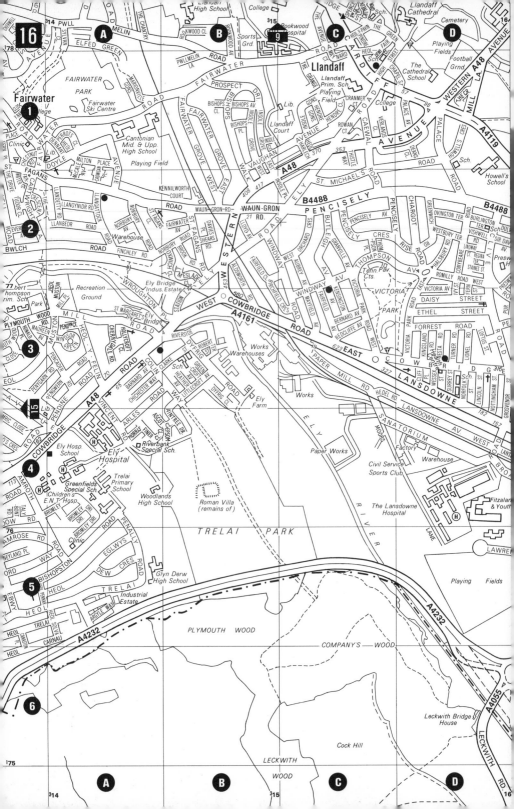

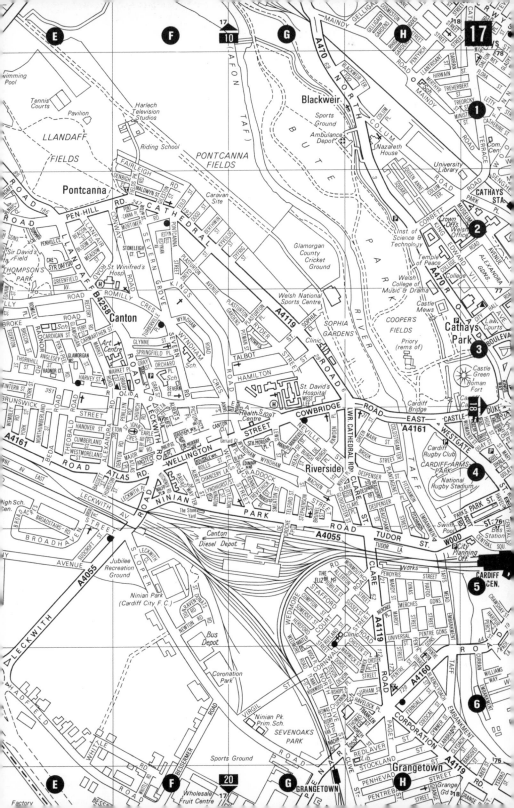

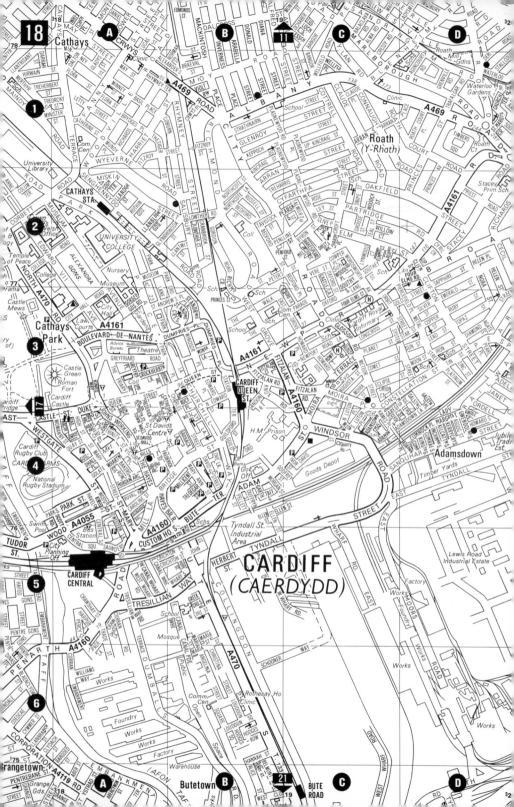

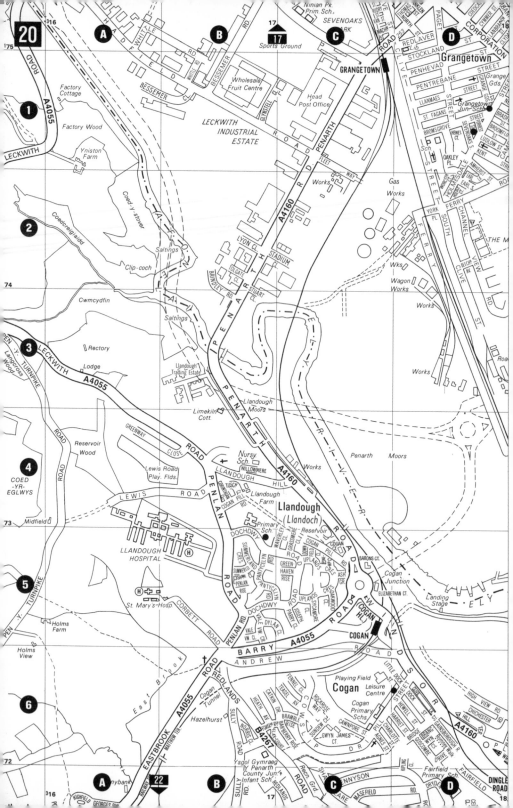

CARDIFF DOCKS

Butetown

A4119

Penarth Head

PENARTH FLATS

The Patch

Cefn-y-wrach

QUEEN ALEXANDRA DOCK

ROATH DOCK

ROATH BASIN

Welsh Indus Maritime Museum

Pier Head

Graving Docks

Channel Oil Works

Customs Waterguard

Pier (Dis.)

Jetties (Disused)

Haulage Depot

TIDAL HARBOUR

Wharf

Landing Stage

Slipway

Subway

Basin

Marine Bldgs.

Headlands School

Royal Hamadryad

Day Nursery

Clarence Bridge

Transit Shed

Transit Shed

Dry Dock

Works

Baths

School

Factory

Warehouse

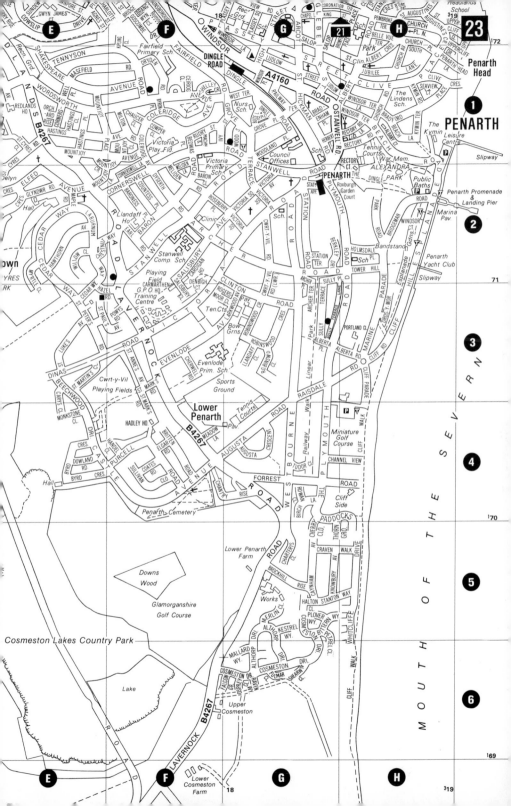

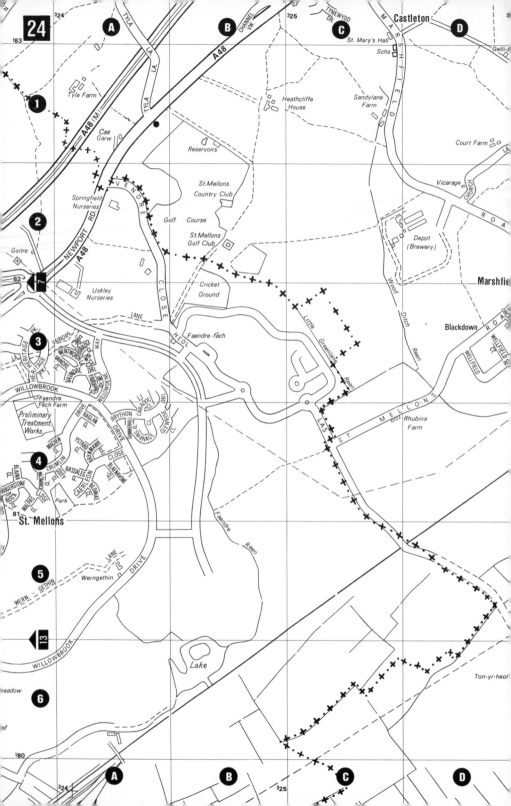

INDEX TO STREETS

HOW TO USE THIS INDEX

(a) A strict alphabetical order is followed in which Av., Rd., St., etc. are read in full and as part of the name preceding them; e.g. Albert Cres. follows Alberta Rd. but precedes Albert Rd.

(b) Each street is followed by its Postal Code District Number and map reference; e.g. Abbey Clo. CF4—2B 2 is in the Cardiff 4 Postal Code District and is to be found in square 2B on page 2.

N.B. The Postal Code District Numbers given in this index are, in fact, only the first part of the Postcode to each address and are only meant to indicate the Postal Code District in which each street is situated.

ABBREVIATIONS USED IN THIS INDEX

All : Alley
App : Approach
Arc : Arcade
Av : Avenue
Bk : Back
Boulevd : Boulevard
Bri : Bridge
B'way : Broadway
Bldgs : Buildings
CF : Cardiff
Chyd : Churchyard

Cir : Circus
Clo : Close
Comn : Common
Cotts : Cottages
Ct : Court
Cres : Crescent
Dri : Drive
E : East
Embkmt : Embankment
Est : Estate
Gdns : Gardens

Ga : Gate
Gt : Great
Grn : Green
Gro : Grove
Ho : House
Junct : Junction
La : Lane
Lit : Little
Lwr : Lower
Mans : Mansions
Mkt : Market

M : Mews
Mt : Mount
N : North
Pal : Palace
Pde : Parade
Pk : Park
Pas : Passage
Pl : Place
Prom : Promenade
Rd : Road
S : South

Sq : Square
Sta : Station
St : Street
Ter : Terrace
Up : Upper
Vs : Villas
Wlk : Walk
W : West
Yd : Yard

Abbey Clo. CF4—2B 2
Aberbran Rd. CF4—5A 10
Abercynon St. CF1—1E 21
Aberdaron Rd. CF3—2F 13
Aberdore Rd. CF4—5A 10
Aberdovey Clo. CF6—2C 22
Aberdovy St. CF2—4E 19
Aberdulais Cres. CF4—5H 9
Aberdulais Rd. CF4—5H 9
Abergele Clo. CF3—1G 13
Abergele Rd. CF3—2F 13
Aberporth Rd. CF4—4H 9
Aber. St. CF1—1E 21
Aberteifi Clo. CF4—5A 10
Aberteifi Cres. CF4—5A 10
Aberthaw Rd. CF5—4G 15
Aberystwith St. CF2—4E 19
Adamsdown La. CF2—4C & 4D 18
Adamsdown Pl. CF2—4D 18
Adamsdown Sq. CF2—4C 18
Adam St. CF1—4B 18
Addison Cres. CF5—4G 15
Adelaide Pl. CF1—1F 21
Adelaide St. CF1—1F 21
Adeline St. CF2—3D 18
Ael-y-Bryn. NF3—3H 11
Ael-y-Bryn CF4—5H 9
Africa Gdns. CF4—5C 10
Agate St. CF2—3D 18
Agincourt Rd. CF2—1D 18
Agnes Rd. CF6—6C 20
Aintree Dri. CF5—4B 16
Albany Ct. CF6—1H 23
Albany Rd. CF2—1E 18
Alberta Pl. CF6—3G 23
Alberta Rd. CF6—3H 23
Albert Cres. CF6—1H 23
Albert St. CF1—4F 17
 (in two parts)
Albert St. La. CF1—4F 17
Albert Wlk. CF1—4F 17
Alderbrook Clo. CF2—4H 5
Alder Rd. CF2—5F 11
Alderwood Clo. CF3—6G 7
Aldsworth Rd. CF5—4B 16
Alexander St. CF2—1A 18
Alexandra Rd. CF5—4E 17
Alfreda Rd. CF4—3F 9
Alfred's Ter. CF4—2A 2
Alfred St. CF2—2E 19
Alice St. CF1—1F 21
Allan Durst Clo. CF4—5D 8
Allen Ct. CF2—1G 11
Allensbank Cres. CF4—5D 10
Allensbank Rd. CF4—5D 10
Allerton St. CF1—5G 17
Alltmawr Rd. CF2—1G 11
Allt Wen CF4—5F 3
Alma Rd. CF2—6G 11
Althorp Dri. CF6—6G 23
Amber Clo. CF3—4B 6

Ambergate Dri. CF3—5B 6
Amberley Clo. CF3—5B 6
Ambleside Av. CF2—5E 11
Amesbury Rd. CF2—6H 11
Amethyst Rd. CF5—6D 8
Amherst St. CF1—1D 20
Amroth Rd. CF5—4H 15
Anchor St. CF4—2A 2
Andrew Rd. CF6—6B 20
Andrews Arc. CF1—3A 18
Andrew's Rd. CF5—5F 9
Angelina St. CF1—6B 18
Angle Pl. CF4—4B 4
Anglesey St. CF2—6G 11
Angus St. CF2—6G 11
Anne St. CF1—4F 17
Anstee Ct. CF5—4F 17
Appledore Rd. CF4—4A 10
Arabella St. CF2—1E 18
Archer Cres. CF5—3H 15
Archer Pl. CF5—6D 8
Archer Pl. CF6—2G 23
Archer Rd. CF5—3F 15
Archer Rd. CF6—2F 23
Archer Ter. CF5—3H 15
Archer Ter. CF6—3G 23
Arcot La. N. CF6—6E 21
Arcot St. CF6—6E 21
Ardwyn CF4—5F 3
Argyle Way CF5—5A 16
Arles Rd. CF5—4A 16
Arlington Cres. CF3—1E 13
Arnold Av. CF3—5E 7
Arnside Rd. CF2—5G 11
Arran Pl. CF2—1E 18
Arran St. CF2—2B & 1C 18
Arthur St. CF2—2E 19
Ascot Clo. CF5—4A 16
Asgog St. CF2—4D 18
Ashburton St. CF2—2E 19
Ashby Rd. CF6—6A 22
Ashcroft Cres. CF5—6B 8
Ashdene Clo. CF5—5D 8
Ashfield Ct. CF3—6G 7
Ash Gro. CF4—1G 9
Ashgrove CF6—3B 22
 (Dinas Powis)
Ash Gro. CF6—5C 20
 (Llandough)
Ash Pl. CF5—1H 15
Ash Tree Clo. CF4—1A 8
Ashwood Ct. CF2—2C 18
Aspen Clo. CF3—6G 7
Athelstan Rd. CF4—3F 9
Atlas Pl. CF5—4F 17
Atlas Rd. CF5—4E 17
Aubrey Av. CF5—2C 16
Augusta Cres. CF6—4G 23
Augusta Rd. CF6—4G 23
Augusta St. CF2—3C 18
Austen Ct. CF3—5F 7
Australia Rd. CF4—5C 10
Avenue Industrial Pk. CF3—5C 6

Avenue, The CF3—5E 13
Avenue, The CF4—3F 9
Avenue, The CF5—6G 9
Avoca Pl. CF1—6G 17
Avondale Cres. CF1—1E 21
Avondale Gdns. CF1—1E 21
Avondale Rd. CF1—1E 21
Avonmuir Rd. CF2—1F 19
Avonridge CF4—3B 4
Awel Mor. CF3—4H 9
Axbridge Cres. CF3—1F 13
Axminster Rd. CF2—1E 19
Azalea Clo. CF2—6H 5

Bacton Rd. CF4—5H 9
Bader Clo. CF4—1D 10
Bakers Row CF1—1A 18
Balaclava Rd. CF2—6G 11
Bala Rd. CF4—5G 9
Ball Clo. CF3—6D 6
Ball La. CF3—1C 12
Ball Rd. CF3—1D 12
Balmoral Clo. CF4—3F 5
Bampton Rd. CF3—6E 7
Banastre Av. CF4—5C 10
Bangor St. CF2—6G 11
Banwell Pl. CF3—1E 13
Barberry Rise CF6—6C 20
Barbrook Clo. CF4—3E 5
Bardsey Cres. CF4—4B 4
Bargoed St. CF1—6A 18
Barmouth Rd. CF4—4D 12
Barnard Av. CF5—3A 16
Barnstaple Rd. CF3—1E 13
Barnwood Cres. CF5—5D 14
Baron Clo. CF6—2F 23
Baroness Pl. CF6—2F 23
Baron Rd. CF6—2F 23
Barons Ct. CF6—5C 20
Baron's Ct. Rd. CF3—5H 11
Barrack La. CF1—4B 18
Barrington Rd. CF4—3H 9
Barry Rd. CF6—6B 20
Basil Pl. CF2—1A 18
Bassaleg Clo. CF3—4A 24
Bassett St. CF1—4E 17
Beach La. CF6—1H 26
Beach Rd. CF6—1H 26
Beacon St. CF1—2E 17
Beale Clo. CF5—5E 9
Beatrice Rd. CF4—3H 9
Beatty Av. CF2—2E 11
Beauchamp St. CF1—4H 17
Beaumaris Rd. CF3—4D 12
Beda Rd. CF5—4E 17
Bedavere Clo. CF4—3C 4
Bedford Pl. CF2—3C 18
Bedford St. CF2—2B 18
 (in two parts)
Bedwas Clo. CF3—4A 24
Bedwas Pl. CF6—1F 23
Bedwas St. CF1—6G 17

Beech Ct. CF4—3D 2
Beecher Av. CF1—2D 20
Beechley Dri. CF5—6B 8
Beech Rd. CF5—1F 15
Beech Tree Clo. CF4—1A 8
Beechwood Dri. CF6—3E 23
Beechwood Rd. CF4—1B 2
Began Rd. CF3—3F 7
Belgrave Clo. CF4—2C 4
Belle Vue Cres. CF4—4F 9
Belle Vue Ter. CF6—6F 21
Belmont Wlk. CF1—1F 21
Beresford La. CF2—2E 19
Beresford Rd. CF2—2E 19
Berkley Dri. CF6—2G 23
Bernard Av. CF5—3C 16
Berrymead Rd. CF2—6F 5
Berry Pl. CF5—5D 8
Berthwin St. CF1—2F 17
Bertram St. CF2—2E 19
Bessemer Clo. CF1—1A 20
Bessemer Rd. CF1—1B 20
Bethania Row CF3—1F 13
Bettws-y-coed Rd. CF2—6F 5
Beulah Rd. CF4—6A 4
Beverley Clo. CF4—4E 5
Bideford Rd. CF3—2E 13
Birch Ct. CF4—2D 2
Birchfield Cres. CF5—2B 16
Birchgrove Rd. CF4—3B 10
Birch Hill CF4—4C 2
Birchwood La. CF2—4G 11
Birchwood Rd. CF2—4F 11
Birkdale Clo. CF3—3A 24
Bishops Av. CF5—1B 16
Bishops Clo. CF4—3G 9
Bishops Clo. CF5—1B 16
Bishops Pl. CF4—3G 9
Bishops Pl. CF5—1B 16
Bishops Rd. CF4—3G 9
Bishops St. CF1—6G 17
Bishopston Rd. CF5—5H 15
Bishops Wlk. CF5—1B 16
Bittern Way CF6—5G 23
Blackbirds Way CF5—5F 7
Blackmoor Pl. CF3—1E 13
Black Oak Rd. CF2—5G 5
Blackstone St. CF1—4G 17
Blackweir Ter. CF1—1H 17
Blaenavon Clo. CF3—4A 24
Blaenclydach St. CF1—6H 17
Blaen-y-Coed CF4—1A 8
 (Radyr)
Blaen-y-Coed CF4—5A 4
 (Rhiwbina)
Blagdon Clo. CF3—2D 12
Blaina Clo. CF3—6H 7
Blanche St. CF2—2E 19
Blandon Way CF4—3G 9
Blanthorn Ct. CF4—1F 9
Blenheim Rd. CF2—1C 18

Blethin Clo. CF5—4E 9
Bloom St. CF1—2E 17
Blosse Rd. CF4—5G 9
Blossom Dri. CF4—1E 5
Bluebell Dri. CF3—5F 7
Blue Ho. Rd. CF4—4C 4
Bluff Cove Rd. CF4—2D 4
Boleyn Wlk. CF2—5G 11
Boncath Rd. CF4—5G 9
Booker St. CF2—2E 19
Borrowdale Clo. CF2—5G 11
Borth Rd. CF2—2F 13
Boswell Clo. CF3—5D 6
Boulevard de Nantes CF1—3A 18
Boverton St. CF2—6B 11
Brachdy La. CF3—5D 12
Brachdy Rd. CF3—5D 12
Bracken Pl. CF5—6D 8
Bradenham Pl. CF6—1G 23
Bradford Pl. CF6—1H 23
Bradford St. CF1—1D 20
Bradley St. CF2—2E 19
Braeval St. CF2—1B 18
Bramble Clo. CF5—6B 8
Bramble Rise CF6—6C 20
Brandreth Rd. CF2—5F 11
Brangwyn Clo. CF6—6D 20
Braunton Av. CF3—1E 13
Braunton Cres. CF3—1D 12
Brayford Pl. CF3—5E 7
Brecon St. CF5—3E 17
Brendon Clo. CF3—1E 13
Briar Clo. CF5—1G 15
Briarwood Dri. CF2—6G 5
Bridgeman Rd. CF6—2H 23
Bridge Rd. CF2—6 to 5F 7
Bridge Rd. CF5 & CF4—5F 9
Bridge St. CF1—4B 18
Bridge St. CF5—6G 9
Bridge St. CF6—6D 20
Bridgwater Rd. CF3—1F 13
Brindley Rd. CF1—2B 20
Britannia Rd. CF2—1G 21
Brithdir St. CF2—6D 10
British Legion Dri. CF3—3D 12
Britten Rd. CF4—6F 3
Britway St. CF6—2A 22
Britway Rd. CF6—2A 22
Broadacres CF5—4E 17
Broadhaven CF1—5E 17
Broadlands Clo. CF3—6G 7
Broad Pl. CF1—4E 17
Broadstairs Rd. CF1—4E 17
Broad St. CF1—4D 16
Broadway CF2—2D 18
Brocastle Rd. CF4—1H 9
Brockhill Rise CF6—5G 23
Bromfield Pl. CF6—6F 21
Bromley Dri. CF5—4A 16
Bromsgrove St. CF1—6G 17
Bron Felen CF4—3B 4
Bronte Clo. CF3—5E 7

Bronte Cres. CF3—5E 7
Bronwydd Av. CF2—5G 11
Bronwydd Clo. CF2—5G 11
Bronwydd Rd. CF2—1G 19
Brookfield Dri. CF3—1G 13
Brooklands Ter. CF5—6D 14
Brooklyn Clo. CF4—4G 3
Brook Rd. CF4—3H 9
Brook St. CF5—2B 16
Brookside CF6—2B 22
Brookside Clo. CF4—2B 10
Brook St. CF1—4H 17
Brookvale Dri. CF4—2C 4
Broomfield St. CF1—1D 20
Broom Pl. CF5—1H 15
Browning Clo. CF3—6D 6
Bruce Knight Clo. CF5—5E 9
Bruce St. CF2—6A 11
Brundall Cres. CF5—6E 15
Brunel St. CF1—4G 17
Brunswick St. CF3—3E 17
Bruton Pl. CF5—6G 9
Brydges Pl. CF2—1A 18
Bryn Adar CF4—5F 3
Bryn-awelon Rd. CF2—5G 5
Bryn Bach CF4—5H 3
Brynbala Way CF3—2G 13
Bryn Castell CF4—6B 2
Bryn Celyn CF2—6B 6
Bryn Celyn Rd. CF2—1B 12
Bryncoch CF4—1A 2
Bryncoed CF4—6A 2
Bryncyn CF2—6B 6
Bryn Derwen CF4—6A 2 & 1A 8
Brynderwen Clo. CF2—3G 11
Brynfedw. CF3—2A 12
Bryn Glas. CF4—3B 4
Bryn Golwg. CF4—6B 2
Bryn gwyn Rd. CF2—6G 5
Brynheulog CF2—6B 6
Bryn Heulog CF2—2F 9
Bryn Hyfryd. CF4—6B 2
Brynmawr Clo. CF3—4A 24
Brynnau Rd. CF4—1B 2
Bryn Pinwydden. CF2—5A 6
Bryn Rhosyn. CF4—6A 2
Brynteg. CF4—4G 3
Brynteg Clo. CF2—3G 11
Bryntirion. CF4—5A 4
Bryn-y-Nant. CF3—2B 12
Brython Dri. CF3—4A 24
Buckingham Clo. CF4—3F 5
Bunyan Clo. CF3—5F 7
Burlington Ter. CF5—2D 16
Burnaby St. CF2—3E 19
Burne Jones Clo. CF5—5E 9
Burnham Av. CF5—5E 7 to
    1E 13
Burnside Ct. CF5—1F 15
Burt Pl. CF1—1F 21
Burt St. CF1—2F 21
Bute Cres. CF1—2G 21
Bute Esplanade CF1—2F 21
Bute Pl. CF1—1G 23
Bute St. CF1—5B 18 to 2G 21
Bute St. CF1—4C 2
Bute Ter. CF1—4B 18
Butleigh Av. CF5—2C 16
Bwlch Rd. CF5—2H 15
Byrd Cres. CF6—4E 23
Byron Pl. CF6—1F 23
Byron St. CF2—2C 18

Cadnant Clo. CF4—4B 4
Cadvan Rd. CF5—3F 15
Cadwgan Pl. CF5—2A 16
Caebach Clo. CF5—6D 14
Caedelyn Rd. CF4—1G 9
Cae Garw. CF6—3A 22
Cae-glas Av. CF3—4D 12
Cae-glas Rd. CF3—4D 12
Caegwyn Rd. CF4—3A 10
Caelewis. CF4—4D 2
Cae Maen. CF4—3B 10
Cae Mawr Rd. CF4—6A 4

Caenewydd Clo. CF5—6D 14
Caerau Ct. CF5—5G 15
Caerau Ct. Rd. CF5—5G 15
Caerau La. CF5—6F 15
Caerau Pk. Cres. CF5—5G 15
Caerau Pk. Pl. CF5—5G 15
Caerau Pk. Rd. CF5—5G 15
Caerau Rd. CF5—5G 15
Caer Cady Clo. CF2—3G 11
Caer Castell Pl. CF3—2E 13
Caer Graig. CF4—6A 2
Caerleon Clo. CF3—4A 24
Caerleon Rd. CF4—5B 10
Caerleon Rd. CF6—1C 22
Caernarvon Clo. CF6—2C 22
Caernarvon Way. CF3—2F 13
Cae'r Odyn. CF6—3A 22
Caerphilly Clo. CF6—1C 22
Caerphilly Rd. CF4
    —6B 4 to 3B 10
Cae'r Wenallt CF4—5F 3
Caerwent Rd. CF5—4E 15
Cae Syr Dafydd. CF1—2E 17
Caewal Rd. CF5—1C 16
Cae Yorath. CF4—2H 9
Cairnmuir Rd. CF2—2F 19
Caldicot Rd. CF5—5H 15
Caldy Rd. CF4—4G 9
Camaes Cres. CF3—2G 13
Cambourne Av. CF4—2F 9
Cambria Rd. CF5—6F 15
Cambridge St. CF1—1E 21
Camelot Way. CF4—3B 4
Cameron. St. CF2—2E 19
Camm's Corner. CF6—2B 22
Campion Pl. CF5—5D 8
Camrose Rd. CF5—5H 15
Canada Rd. CF4—6C 10
Canal Pde. CF1—6B 18
Canaston Pl. CF5—5H 15
Cannington Av. CF3—2E 13
Canton Ct. CF1—4F 17
Capelgwilym Rd. CF4—1A 4
Caradoc Clo. CF3—4A 24
Cardiff Rd. CF4—1A 2
Cardiff Rd. CF5—6G 9 to 2E 17
    (Llandaff)
Cardiff Rd. CF5—2E 15
    (St. Fagans)
Cardiff Rd. CF6—5A 22
Cardigan Clo. CF6—2C 22
Cardigan Ho. CF6—2F 23
Cardigan Rd. CF6—2C 22
Cardigan St. CF5—3E 17
Cargo Rd. CF1—3G 21
Carisbrooke Way. CF3—4G 11
Carlisle St. CF2—3E 19
Carlton Clo. CF4—2C 4
Carmarthen Ho. CF6—3F 23
Carmarthen Rd. CF6—2C 22
Carmarthen St. CF5—3E 17
Carnegie Dri. CF2—2F 11
Caroline St. CF1—4A 18
Ca'r Pwll. CF6—3A 22
Carter Pl. CF5—6D 8
Cartwright La. CF5—2H 15
Carys Clo. CF6—3E 23
Castell Coch View. CF4—4C 2
Castle Arc. CF4—4A 18
Castle Av. CF3—5B 12
Castle Av. CF4—4E 23
Castle Cres. CF3—5C 12
Castle Dri. CF6—2C 22
Castlefield Pl. CF4—5C 10
Castle Hill. CF5—2D 14
Castle La. CF2—2C 18
Castle Rd. CF4—3C 2
Castle St. CF1—4H 17
Castle St. CF4—2A 2
Castle View. CF4—5D 2
Castlewood Cotts. CF6—2A 22
Caswell Rd. CF3—4D 12
Cathays Ter. CF2—6A 11
Cath Cob Clo. CF3—1G 13
Cathedral Grn. The.CF5—6G 9
Cathedral Rd. CF1—2F 17
Cathedral View. CF4—5H 9
Cathedral Wlk. CF1—3A 18

Catherine Dri. CF4—3D 2
Catherine St. CF2—1A 18
Catkin Dri. CF6—6B 20
Cawnpore St. CF6—6C 20
Caxton St. CF2—5C 6
Caynham Av. CF6—5G 23
Cecil St. CF2—2D 18
Cedar Gro. CF5—6C 8
Cedar Way. CF6—2E 23
Cefn Carnau Rd. CF4—2D 10
Cefn Coch. CF4—6A 2
Cefn-Coed. CF2—3G 11
Cefn-Coed Cres. CF2—4G 11
Cefn-Coed Gdns. CF2—4F 11
Cefn-Coed Rd. CF2—4F 11
Cefn Graig. CF4—5H 3
Cefn Mably Rd. CF4—2G 5
Cefn Mt. CF6—2A 22
Cefn Nant. CF4—4H 3
Cefn Porth Rd. CF3—1B 6
Cefn Rd. CF4—4A 10
Ceiriog Clo.CF6—1F 23
Ceiriog Dri. CF4—5G 3
Celtic Grn. CF6—1B 22
Celtic Rd. CF4—4B 10
Celyn Av. CF2—2F 11
Celyn Gro. CF2—6G 5
Cemetery Rd. CF4—2B 2
Central Sq. CF1—5A 18
Chamberlain Rd. CF4—4F 9
Chamberlain Row. CF6—1C 22
Chancery La. CF1—4F 17
Channel View. CF3—1B 24
Channel View. CF6—4G 23
Channel View Rd. CF1—2D 20
Chantry Rise. CF6—4F 23
Chantry, The. CF6—6E 9
Chapel Clo. CF6—1C 22
Chapel La. CF6—6E 21
Chapel Rd. CF4—5B 2
Chapel Row. CF6—6F 7
Chapel Row. CF6—1C 22
Chapel St. CF5—1D 16
Chapel Wood. CF3—3A 12
Chard Av. CF3—2D 12
Chargot Rd. CF5—2D 16
Charles St. CF1—3B 18
Charlotte Sq. CF4—6A 4
Charlotte St. CF6—6C 20
Charteris Clo. CF6—5G 23
Charteris Cres. CF5—3H 15
Charteris Rd. CF5—3H 15
Chartwell Dri. CF4—4F 5
Chaucer Clo. CF3—5E 7
Chaucer Clo. CF6—1F 23
Cheam Pl. CF4—5C 4
Cheddar Cres. CF3—2D 12
Chepstow Clo. CF5—5H 15
Cherry Clo. CF5—6B 8
Cherry Clo. CF6—3C 22
    (Dinas Powis)
Cherry Clo. CF6—5G 23
    (Penarth)
Cherrydale Rd. CF5—3A 16
Cherry Orchard Rd. CF4
    —1C 4 & 2E 5
Cherry Tree Clo. CF4—2F 5
Cherwell Clo. CF6—6B 8
Cherwell Rd. CF6—3F 23
Cheshire Clo. CF4—1D 10
Chester Pl. CF1—6H 17
Chester St. CF1—6H 17
Chesterton Rd. CF3—6D 6
Chestnut Clo. CF6—3B 22
Chestnut Rd. CF5—1H 15
Chestnut Tree Clo. CF4—1A 8
Chestnut Way. CF6—2E 23
Cheviot Clo. CF4—6C 4
Chichester Rd. CF6—6D 20
Chichester Way. CF5—3A 16
Chiltern Clo. CF4—6C 4
Christina St. CF1—6B 18
Chulmleigh Clo. CF3—3C 12
Church Av. CF6—1H 26
Church Clo. CF4—3C 5
Churchill Way. CF1—3B 18

Church La. CF3—2D 24
    (Marshfield)
Church La. CF3—6F 7
    (St Mellons)
Church Pl. N. CF6—6F 21
Church Pl. S. CF6—6F 21
Church Rd. CF1—4F 17
Church Rd. CF3—5C 6
    (Llanedeyrn)
Church Rd. CF3—4C 12
    (Rumney)
Church Rd. CF4—2G 5
    (Lisvane)
Church Rd. CF4—3F 9
    (Whitchurch)
Church Rd. CF5—6G 15
Church Rd. CF6—1H 26
Church St. CF1—4A 18
Church St. CF4—2A 2
Church Ter. CF2—1D 18
Cilfedw CF4—6B 2
Cilgerran Cres. CF4—5B 4
Circle Way E. CF3
    —1A 12 to 4A 12
Circle Way W. CF2 & CF3
    —2H & 3H 11
City Hall Rd. CF1—3A 18
City Rd. CF2—1D 18
Claerwen Dri. CF2—2F 11
Clarbeston Rd. CF5—5G 9
Clare Gdns. CF1—4H 17
Claremont Av. CF3—3D 12
Claremont Cres. CF3—3D 12
Clarence Embkmt. CF1—2E 21
Clarence Pl. CF1—2F 21
Clarence Rd. CF1—1E 21
Clarendon Rd. CF3—4H 11
Clare Pl. CF1—4H 17
Clare Rd. CF1—5H 17
Clare St. CF1—4H 17
Clarke St. CF5—3B 16
Clas Canol. CF4—4H 9
Clas Dyfrig. CF4—4H 9
Clas Gabriel CF4—4H 9
Clas Heulog CF4—4H 9
Clas Ifor CF4—2A 10
Clas Illtyd. CF4—3A 10
Clas Isan. CF4—3A 10
Clas Odyn. CF4—4H 9
Clas Teilo. CF4—4H 9
Clas Treoda. CF4—4H 9
Clas Ty'n-y-cae. CF4—1A 10
Clas Tywern. CF4—1A 10
Clas Yorath CF4—2H 9
Claude Pl. CF2—1C 18
Claude Rd. CF2—1C 18
Clearwater Way. CF2—2F 11
Clevedon Rd. CF3—1D 12
Cleve Dri. CF4—6C 4
Cliff Hill. CF6—3H 23
Cliff Pde. CF6—3H 23
Cliff Pl. CF5—3D 16
Cliff Rd. CF6—3H 23
Cliff St. CF6—6F 21
Cliff Wlk. CF6—6H to 4H 23
Clifton St. CF2—2C 18
Clinton Rd. CF6—3G 23
Clipper Rd. CF1—6F 19
Clive Cres. CF6—1H 26
Clive La. CF6—6D 20
Clive Pl. CF2—2C 18
Clive Pl. CF6—6H 21
Clive Rd. CF5—2D 16
Clive St. CF1—1D 20
Clodien Av. CF4—5D 10
Clos Brynderi. CF4—6A 4
Clos Bryn Melyn. CF4—1B 8
Clos Coedydafarn CF4—3F 5
Clos Cornel. CF4—3H 9
Clos Cromwell. CF4—4A 4
Close, The. CF4—5D 4
Clos Fach. CF4—5B 4
Clos Hendre. CF4—5B 4
Clos Mabon. CF4—5H 3
Clos Ton Mawr. CF4—4A 4
Clos William. CF4—4A 4
Clos y Bryn. CF4—4G 3
Clos y Craig. CF4—4H 3

Clos-y-Nant. CF5—1H 15
Clos yr Aer. CF4—5A 4
Clos yr Hafod. CF4—5A 4
Clos yr Wenallt. CF4—4H 3
Clos y Wenex. CF4—5A 4
Clovelly Cres. CF3—2C 12
Clover Clo. CF5—6C 8
Clun Ter. CF2—5E 11
Clydach St. CF1—6H 17
Clydesmuir Industrial Est. CF2
    —1F 19
Clydesmuir Rd. CF2—2F 19
Clyde St. CF2—4C 18
Clyro Pl. CF4—4G 9
Coates Pl. CF3—6F 7
Coates Rd. CF6—4F 23
Coburn St. CF2—1B 18
Coed Arhyd. CF5—5C 14
Coedcae St. CF1—6H 17
Coed Cochwyn Av. CF4—4C 4
Coeden Dal. CF2—5A 6
Coed Glas Rd. CF4—5B 4
Coed Edeyrn. CF3—3H 11
Coedydafarn. CF4—3G 5
Coed-y-Gloriau. CF2—6H 5
Coed-y-Gores. CF3—2A 12
Coed-y-Llyn. CF2—3F 11
Coed-y-Llyn. CF4—6A 2
Coed yr Ynn. CF4—5A 4
Cogan Ct. CF6—5C 20
Cogan Hill. CF6—5C 20
Cogan Pill Rd. CF6—4B & 5C 20
Cogan Ter. CF2—2A 18
Cog Rd. CF6—6C 22
Coity Clo. CF3—4A 24
Colbourne Wlk. CF1—4F 17
Colchester Av. CF3—6H11
Colchester Factory Est. CF3
    —6A 12
Coldstream Ter. CF1—4H 17
Coleridge Av. CF6—1F 23
Colin Parsons Clo. CF4—2D 4
Colin Way. CF5—3A 16
College Clo. CF4—2H 17
College Rd. CF4—5G to 3H 9
Collingdon Rd. CF1—5B 18
Colum Pl. CF1—1H 17
Colum Rd. CF1—1H 17
Colum Ter. CF1—2H 17
Colwill Rd. CF4—5H 9
Colwinstone Clo. CF4—4G 9
Colwinstone St. CF4—4G 9
Colwyn Rd. CF3—3D 12
Comet St. CF2—3C 18
Compass Rd. CF1—2H 21
Compton St. CF1—1D 20
Connaught Rd. CF2—1C 18
Constellation St. CF2—3C 18
Conway Clo. CF6—2C 22
Conway Rd. CF1—2F 17
Conybeare Rd. CF5—2D 16
Copleston Rd. CF4—5G 9
Copperfield Dri. CF4—3D 4
Copper St. CF2—3D 18
Coppins, The. CF4—2F 5
Corbett La. CF1—2H 17
Corbett Rd. CF6—5B 20
Corinthian Clo. CF6—4B 20
Cormorant Clo. CF3—5H 7
Cornelly Clo. CF4—4G 9
Cornelly St. CF4—4G 9
Cornerswell Pl. CF6—1E 23
Cornerswell Pl. CF6—1E 23
Cornerswell Rd. CF6—2F 23
Cornfield Clo. CF4—4B 4
Cornflower Clo. CF4—1E 5
Cornwall St. CF1—6G 17
Coronation Rd. CF4—3B 10
Coronation Ter. CF6—6E 21
Corporation Rd. CF1—6H 17
Corwen Cres. CF4—4G 9
Coryton Clo. CF4—6E 3
Coryton Cres. CF4—6E 3
Coryton Dri. CF4—6E 3
Coryton Rise. CF4—6E 3
Cosheston Rd. CF5—5D 8
Cosmeston Dri. CF6—6G 23
Cosmeston St. CF2—6D 10

Cosslett Pl. CF1—1E 21
Cotswold Av. CF4—2F 5
Cottrell Rd. CF2—1C 18
Cottrell Rd. CF4—3H 9
Countess Pl. CF4—4A 10
Countisbury Av. CF3—1E 13
Court Clo. CF4—4A 10
Courtenay Rd. CF3—3E 19
Courtis Rd. CF5—4F 15
Court Rd. CF1—5G 17
Court Rd. CF4—4A 10
Coveny St. CF2—3E 19
Cowbridge Rd. E. CF5—3B 16 to
4H 17
Cowbridge Rd. W. CF5—6E 15
to 3B 16
Cowper Clo. CF6—1F 23
Cowper Pl. CF2—2C 18
Cowslip Dri. CF6—6C 20
Craddock St. CF1—4G 17
Cradoc Rd. CF4—3A 10
Craigmuir Rd. CF2—2F 19
Cranbrook St. CF2—2B 18
Cranleigh Rise. CF3—3C 12
Cranmer Ct. CF5—1C 16
Craven Wlk. CF6—5G 23
Crawley Clo. CF4—2C4
Crawshay La. CF1—5A 18
Crawshay St. CF1—5A 18
Crediton Rd. CF3—1E 13
Crescent, The. CF5—2H 15
(Fairwater)
Crescent, The. CF5—1D 16
(Llandaff)
Cressy Rd. CF2—6G 11
Criccieth Ct. CF6—1C 22
Criccieth Rd. CF3—4E 13
Crichton Pl. CF1—5A 18
Crichton St. CF1—5B 18
Crickhowell Rd. CF3—1G 13
Crockhertown La. CF1—3A 18
Croescadarn Rd. CF3—3B 6
Croffta. CF6—3A 22
Crofft-y-genau Rd. CF5—1D 14
Crofta, The. CF4—4F 5
Croft St. CF2—2C 18
Cromwell Rd. CF6—3B 22
Cross Comn. Rd. CF6—3B 22
Cross Pl. CF4—4C 2
Cross St. CF4—4C 2
Crossways Rd. CF5—4G 15
Crown Way. CF4—6C 10
Croyde Av. CF3—1E 13
Crumlin Dri. CF3—6H 7
Crundale Cres. CF4—6D 4
Crwys Pl. CF2—1B 18
Crwys Rd. CF2—6A 11
Crystal Av. CF2—1E 11
Crystal Glen. CF4—1D 10
Crystal Rise. CF4—1D 10
Crystal Wood Rd. CF4—1D 10
Cumberland St. CF5—4E 17
Cumnock Pl. CF2—4D 18
Cumnock Ter. CF2—4D 18
Cumrae St. CF2—4D 18
Cunningham Clo. CF2—3E 11
Curlew Clo. CF4—1G 9
Curll Av. CF2—2E 19
Curran Embkmt. CF1—6A 18
Curran Rd. CF1—5A 18
Custom Ho. St. CF1—5A 18
Cwmcarn Clo. CF3—6H 7
Cwmdare St. CF2—6D 10
Cwm Nofydd. CF4—5H 3
Cwrt Cefn. CF4—3E 5
Cwrt Ty-Mynydd. CF4—1B 8
Cwrt-yr-Ala Av. CF5—6F 15
Cwrt-yr-Ala Rd. CF5—6F 15
Cwrt-y-Vil Rd. CF6—2G 23
Cwrt-y-Vil Rd. (Lwr.) CF6
—3G 23
Cyfarthfa St. CF2—2C 18
Cymmer St. CF1—6H 17
Cymric Clo. CF5—4H 15
Cyncoed Av. CF2—1G 11
Cyncoed Cres. CF2—1G 11
Cyncoed Pl. CF2—1G 11
Cyncoed Rise. CF2—1G 11

Cyncoed Rd. CF2—5G 5 to 5H 11
Cyntwell Av. CF5—6F 15
Cyntwell Cres. CF5—6F 15
Cyntwell Pl. CF5—5F 15
Cypress Pl. CF6—6D 8
Cyril Cres. CF2—2D 18

Daisy St. CF5—3D 16
Dalcross St. CF2—6B 11
Dale Av. CF4—2B 10
Dalmuir Rd. CF2—2F 19
Dalton St. CF2—1A 18
Danescourt Way. CF5—5D 8
Daniel St. CF2—6A 11
Dan-y-Bryn Av. CF4—1A 8
Dan-y-Bryn Clo. CF4—1B 8
Dan-y-coed Clo. CF2—1F 11
Dan-y-coed Rise. CF2—1F 11
Dan-y-Graig. CF4—5F 3
Dan-yr-Heol. CF2—1H 17
Darran St. CF2—1H 17
David St. CF1—4B 18
Davies Pl. CF4—3A 10
Daviot St. CF2—6B 11
Davis St. CF1—4C 18
Deans Clo. CF5—1D 16
De Burgh Pl. CF1—4G 17
De Burgh St. CF1—4G 17
De Croche Pl. CF1—5G 17
Deemuir Rd. CF2—2F 19
Deepdale Clo. CF2—4F 11
Deepfield Clo. CF5—4D 14
Deepwood Clo. CF5—4D 14
Deere Clo. CF5—5F 15
Deere Pl. CF5—5F 15
Deere Rd. CF5—5E 15
Deganwy Clo. CF4—4C 4
Dell, The. CF3—5F 7
Delta St. CF1—4F 17
Denbigh Ct. CF6—2F 23
Denbigh Rd. CF6—1C 22
Denbigh St. CF1—2F 17
Denison Way. CF5—4D 14
Den Roche Pl. CF1—3B 18
Denton Rd. CF5—4F 17
Denys Clo. CF6—1B 22
Deri Rd. CF2—1D 18
Derwen Rd. CF2—3C 5
Derwent Clo. CF4—3C 4
Despenser Gdns. CF1—4H 17
Despenser Pl. CF1—4H 17
Despenser St. CF1—4H 17
Dessmuir Rd. CF2—2F 19
Devon Pl. CF1—6G 17
Devon St. CF1—6G 17
Dew Cres. CF5—5A 16
Dewi St. CF5—1C 16
Diamond St. CF2—3D 18
Diana La. CF2—6B 11
Diana St. CF2—6B 11
Dickens Av. CF3—6D 6
Digby Clo. CF4—5E 9
Dinas Pl. CF1—6H 17
Dinas Rd. CF6—3E 23
Dinas St. CF1—5H 17
Dingle La. CF6—1G 23
Dingle Rd. CF6—1G 23
Dingle, The. CF6—2H 23
Dochdwy Rd. CF6—5B 20
Dock Rd. CF6—6F 21
Dock St. CF6—6D 20
Dogfield St. CF2—6A 11
Dogo St. CF1—2F 17
Dolgoch Clo. CF3—3F 13
Dolwen Rd. CF4—5G 9
Dombey Clo. CF4—3D 4
Dominions Arc. CF1—3A 18
Dominion Way. CF2—1E 19
Donald St. CF2—6B 11
Dorchester Av. CF3—5H 11
Dorset St. CF1—6G 17
Douglas Clo. CF5—5E 9
Dovedale Clo. CF4—4F 11
Dovey Clo. CF3—2F 13
Dowland Rd. CF5—6E 9
Downfield Clo. CF5—5C 20
Downlands Way. CF3—5C 12

Downton La. CF3—5D 12
Downton Rise. CF3—5D 12
Doyle Av. CF5—1A 16
Drawlings Clo. CF3—5F 7
Drive, The. CF2—2H 15
Drive, The. CF6—2C 22
Drope Rd. CF5—5C 14
Dros-y-Mor. CF6—3H 23
Dros-y-Morfa. CF3—5E 13
Druidstone Rd. CF3—4G 7
Dryburgh Av. CF4—2B 10
Dryden Clo. CF3—6D 6
Dryden Rd. CF6—1F 23
Drylla. CF6—3A 22
Drysgol Rd. CF4—1B 8
Dudley Ct. CF2—2F 21
Dudley Pl. CF2—2F 21
Dudley St. CF1—2F 21
Duffryn Av. CF2—2F 11
Duffryn Clo. CF2—1E 11
Duffryn Rd. CF2—1G 11
Duffryn St. CF1—4B 18
Dugdale Wlk. CF1—4F 17
Duke St. CF1—4A 18
Duke St. Arc. CF1—4A 18
Dulverton Av. CF3—1E 13
Dulwich Gdns. CF5—2D 16
Dumballs Rd. CF1—6A 18
Dumfries Pl. CF1—3B 18
Dunkery Clo. CF3—2D 12
Dunraven Clo. CF6—2C 22
Dunraven Rd. CF1—5F 17
Dunsmuir Rd. CF2—3F 19
Dunster Rd. CF3—1F 13
Durham St. CF1—6H 17
Durleigh Clo. CF3—6E 7
Durlston Clo. CF4—4F 9
Duxford Clo. CF5—5D 8
Dyfrig Clo. CF5—3B 16
Dyfrig Rd. CF5—3B 16
Dyfrig St. CF2—1G 17
Dylan Clo. CF6—5B 20
Dylan St. CF2—2C 18
Dynevor Rd. CF3—4H 11
Dyserth Rd. CF1—6H 17

Earle Pl. CF5—4F 17
Earl La. CF1—2D 20
Earl Rd. CF6—2F 23
Earl's Ct. Pl. CF3—6H 11
Earl's Ct. Rd. CF3—5H 11
Earl St. CF1—2D 20
Eastbrook Clo. CF6—1B 22
Eastbrook Rd. CF6—6A 20
E. Canal Wharf. CF1
—5A & 5B 18
Eastern Av. CF4, CF2 & CF3
—5B 10 to 3G 7
Eastern Clo. CF3—5F 7
East Gro. CF2—3C 18
East Gro. La. CF2—3C 18
E. Moors Rd. CF1—5D 18
E. Rise. CF4—5E 5
E. Tyndall St. CF1—4D 18
Ebwy Ct. CF5—5H 15
Eclipse St. CF2—3C 18
Edgehill Av. CF4—4A 4
Edinburgh Maisonettes CF1
—4G 17
Edington Av. CF4—5D 10
Edith Rd. CF6—2B 22
Edmonds Ct. CF2—3C 18
Edward Clarke Clo. CF5—5E 9
Edward Nicholl Ct. CF3—5H 11
Edward Pl. CF1—3A 18
Egerton St. CF5—3E 17
Egham St. CF5—3E 17
Egremont Rd. CF2—4F 11
Eider Clo. CF3—6G 7
Elaine Clo. CF3—6C 4
Elan Rd. CF4—6E 5
Elderberry Rd. CF5—6B 8
Elder Wood Clo. CF3—4A 12
Eleanor Pl. CF1—2E 21
Elfed Av. CF6—2E 23
Elfed Grn. CF5—6E 9
Elford Rd. CF5—4G 15
Elgar Cres. CF3—6F 7

Elgar Rd. CF6—4F 23
Elizabethan Ct. CF6—5C 20
Elizabeth Maisonettes, The. CF1
—5G 17
Ellen St. CF1—4B 18
Ellesmere Ct. CF3—1F 13
Elmfield Clo. CF3—1G 13
Elm Gro. La. CF6—2A 22
Elm Gro. Pl. CF6—2B 22
Elmgrove Rd. CF4—3E 9
Elm Gro. Rd. CF6—2A 22
Elm St. CF2—2C 18
Elmwood Ct. CF2—2C 18
Ely Bridge Industrial Est. CF5
—2A 16
Ely Rd. CF5—2B 16
Emerald St. CF2—3D 18
Ennerdale Clo. CF2—5F 11
Epsom Clo. CF5—4B 16
Epstein Clo. CF5—5D 8
Erw Las. CF4—3G 9
Erw'r Delyn Clo. CF6—1D 22
Erw Wen. CF4—5H 3
Eskdale Clo. CF4—4F 9
Esplanade. CF6—2H 23
Essich St. CF2—6A 11
Ethel St. CF5—3D 16
Eton Pl. CF5—4F 17
Eurwg Cres. CF3—5F 7
Evansfield Rd. CF4—4F 9
Evelyn St. CF1—1F 21
Evenlode Av. CF6—3F 23
Everard Way. CF2—3F 11
Everest Av. CF4—4D 4
Everest Wlk. CF4—4D 4
Everswell Av. CF2—2H 15
Everswell Rd. CF5—2H 15
Ewenny Rd. CF4—6E 5
Excalibur Dri. CF4—3B 4
Exford Cres. CF3—2C 12
Eyre St. CF2—3E 19

Fairbrook Clo. CF4—5H 3
Fairfax Rd. CF4—1B 10
Fairfield Av. CF5—3C 16
Fairfield Clo. CF5—2B 16
Fairfield Rd. CF6—1F 23
Fairhaven Clo. CF3—3A 24
Fairleigh Rd. CF1—1F 17
Fairoak Ct. CF2—5F 11
Fairoak Rd. CF2—6A 11
Fairoaks. CF6—2B 22
Fairview Clo. CF3—3A 24
Fairview Ct. CF2—6H 5
Fairwater Av. CF5—2B 16
Fiarwater Grn. CF5—2H 15
Fairwater Gro. E. CF5—1B 16
Fairwater Gro. W. CF5—1B 16
Fairwater Rd. CF5—1H 15
Fairways Cres. CF5—2G 15
Fairway, The. CF2—4G 5
Fairwood Rd. CF5—6E 9
Falcon Gro. CF6—6G 23
Falconwood Dri. CF5—5D 14
Fanny St. CF2—1A 18
Farm Dri. CF2—3F 11
Farmhouse Way. CF5—6F 15
Farmleigh. CF3—4D 12
Farmville Rd. CF2—3E 19
Felin Fach. CF4—4H 9
Felin Wen. CF4—6A 4
Fennel Clo. CF6—6C 20
Ferndale St. CF1—6H 17
Fern Pl. CF5—1H 15
Fern St. CF5—3D 16
Ferntree Dri. CF3—6G 7
Ferny Ct. CF3—5H 11
Ferrier Av. CF5—1H 15
Ferry La. CF6—6F 21
Ferry Rd. CF1—2D 20
(in two parts)
Ferry Rd. CF1—2E 21
(Butetown)
Festiniog Rd. CF4—5G 9
Ffordd-Las. CF4—1A 8
Fidlas Av. CF4—6E 5
Fidlas Rd. CF4—5D 4
Fielding Clo. CF3—6D 6

Fields Pk. Rd. CF1—2F 17
Finchley Rd. CF5—2A 16
Firs Av. CF5—1F 15
Firwood Clo. CF4—3F 9
Fishguard Clo. CF4—6E 5
Fishguard Rd. CF4—6D 4
Fishpond Rd. CF3—1D 12
Fitzalan Ct. CF2—3B 18
Fitzalan Pl. CF2—3B 18
Fitzalan Rd. CF2—3B & 3C 18
Fitzhamon Embkmt. CF1—
4H 17
Fitzhamon La. CF1—4H 17
Fitzroy St. CF2—1A & 1B 18
Flax Ct. CF6—6B 20
Flaxland Av. CF4—4C 10
Fleet Way. CF1—1C 20
Flint St. CF4—6C 10
Flora St. CF2—1A 18
(in two parts)
Florence St. CF2—2E 19
Florentia St. CF2—6A 11
Fonmon Cres. CF5—4H 15
Fontigary Rd. CF3—4E 13
Foreland Rd. CF4—2G 9
Forest Farm Rd. CF4—1D 8
Forest Oak Clo. CF2—4G 5
Forest View. CF5—2G 15
Forge St. CF5—5F 15
Forrest Rd. CF5—3D 16
Forrest Rd. CF6—4G 23
Forrest St. CF1—1D 20
Forsythia Dri. CF2—6H 5
Fort St. CF2—2E 19
Four Elms Ct. CF2—3C 18
Four Elms Rd. CF2—2D 18
Foxglove Clo. CF5—5F 15
Foxglove Rise. CF6—6B 20
Fox St. CF2—2E 19
Franklen Rd. CF4—3A 10
Franklen St. CF1—6H 17
Frank Rd. CF5—3G 15
Frederick St. CF1—3A & 4A 18
Fremington Pl. CF3—2E 13
Freshmoor Rd. CF2—4E 19
Frewer Av. CF5—6D 8
Friary, The. CF1—3A 18
Frigate Rd. CF1—1H 21
Fulmar Clo. CF3—6G 7
Fulmar Clo. CF6—6G 23
Furness Clo. CF5—5E 15

Gabalfa Av. CF4—5G 9
Gabalfa Rd. CF4—5B 4
Gaerwen Clo. CF4—5B 4
Gainsborough Rd. CF6—6D 20
Galahad Clo. CF4—4B 4
Gallamuir Rd. CF2—2F 19
Galston Pl. CF2—3D 18
Galston St. CF2—3D 18
Gardenia Clo. CF2—6H 5
Garesfield St. CF2—4C 18
Gareth Clo. CF3—3B 4
Garth Clo. CF4—6A 4
Garth Pl. CF4—5B 10
Garth St. CF1—4B 18
Garth St. CF4—2A 2
Gawain Clo. CF4—3B 4
Gelli Deg. CF4—5H 3
Gelligaer Gdns. CF2—6D 10
Gelligaer St. CF2—6D 10
Gelynis Ter. CF4—5B 2
Gelynis Ter. N. CF4—5B 2
Georges Row. CF6—1C 22
George St. CF1—1G 21
Georgian Way. CF4—5D 4
Geraint Clo. CF4—3B 4
Gernant. CF4—6A 4
Gerrard Ct. CF1—4F 17
Gibson Clo. CF4—1D 10
Gilbert Pl. CF4—5A 10
Gileston St. CF1—2F 17
Gilian Rd. CF5—6F 9
Gilwern Cres. CF4—4C 4
Gilwern Pl. CF4—4C 4
Gladys St. CF2—1A 18
Glamorgan M. CF5—3E 17

27

Glamorgan St. CF5—3E 17
Glandovey Gro. CF3—1G 13
Glandwr Pl. CF4—3H 9
Glan Ely Clo. CF5—2G 15
Glanmuir Rd. CF2—1G 19
Glanrhyd. CF4—6A 4
Glan-y-Fford. CF4—1A 2
Glan-y-mor Rd. CF3—2G 13
Glan-y-Nant Ter. CF4—2H 9
Glas Efail. CF4—6B 4
Glastonbury Ter. CF3—2D 12
Glas-y-Pant. CF4—6F 3
Glebe Pl. CF4—5D 4
Glebe St. CF6—6E 21
Glendale Av. CF4—4C 4
Glenrise Clo. CF3—4A 24
Glenroy St. CF2—1B 18
Glen View. CF4—1D 10
Glenwood. CF2—1H 11
Glossop Rd. CF2—3C 18
Glossop Ter. CF2—3C 18
Gloucester St. CF1—4G 17
Glyn Coed Rd. CF2—6A 6
Glyn Collen. CF2—6C 6
Glyndwr Rd. CF5—3F 15
Glyndwr Rd. CF6—2E 23
Glyn Eiddew. CF2—5B 6
Glynne St. CF1—3F 17
Glynrhondda St. CF2—2A 18
Glyn Rhosyn. CF2—5H 5
Glyn Simon Clo. CF4—4E 9
Glynstell Clo. CF1—1B 20
Glyn Thomas Clo. CF4—3D 4
Godfrey St. CF1—4B 18
Golate. CF1—4A 18
Goldcrest Dri. CF2—6H 5
Goldsmith Clo. CF3—6D 6
Gold St. CF2—3D 18
Goodwick Rd. CF3—4E 13
Goodwood Clo. CF5—5D 14
Gordon Rd. CF2—2B 18
Gorsedd Gdns. Rd. CF1—3A 18
Gorse Pl. CF5—1G 15
Goscombe Dri. CF6—6D 20
Gough Rd. CF5—4G 15
Gower St. CF2—6A 11
Grafton Clo. CF3—4H 11
Grafton Ter. CF4—1A 10
Graham Wlk. CF1—4F 17
Graig Castell. CF4—6B 2
Graig Hir. CF4—6B 2
Graig Llwyd. CF4—6B 2
Graig-Llwyn Rd. CF4—1G 5
Graig Rd. CF4—1F 5
Graig View. CF4—2F 5
Graig Wen. CF4—5B 2
Graig yr Allt. CF4—4H 3
Grand Av. CF5—5E 15
Grange Gdns. CF1—1D 20
Grange Pl. CF1—1E 21
Grange, The. CF5—1C 16
Grant's Clo. CF4—5C 2
Granville Av. CF5—2C 16
Grasmere Av. CF2—4E 11
Grasmere Clo. CF6—5C 20
Gray La. CF1—3F 17
Gray St. CF1—3F 17
Gt. Western La. CF1—4A 18
Greek Church St. CF1—5B 18
Greenclose Rd. CF4—3A 10
Greencroft Av. CF5—3B 16
Green Farm Clo. CF5—5E 15
Green Farm Rd. CF5—5E 15
Greenfield Av. CF1—2E 17
Greenfield Av. CF4—2A 10
Greenfield Av. CF6—2A 22
Greenfield Rd. CF4—2A 10
Greenhaven Rise. CF6—5C 20
Greenland Cres. CF5—1G 15
Greenlawns. CF2—5H 11
Greenmeadow Clo. CF6—3B 22
Greenmeadow Dri. CF4—4D 2
Greenmeadows. CF3—2G 13
Greenock Rd. CF3—2F 13
Green St. CF1—4H 17
Green, The. CF4—2C 8
Green, The. CF5—6G 9
Greenway Av. CF3—4E 13

Greenway Clo. CF6—4A 20
Greenway Rd. CF3—4E 13 to
6G 7
Greenwich Rd. CF5—2D 16
Greenwood La. CF5—2E 15
Greenwood Rd. CF5—6F 9
Grenville Rd. CF2—1D 18
Gresford Clo. CF3—1F 13
Greyfriars Pl. CF1—3A 18
Greyfriars Rd. CF1—3A 18
Greylands, The. CF4—1A 10
Grisedale Clo. CF2—5F 11
Groes Lon. CF4—5H 3
Gron Fford. CF4—4H 3
Grosvenor St. CF5—4D 16
Grouse St. CF2—2C 18
Groveland Rd. CF4—3B 10
Grove Pl. CF4—2B 10
Grove Pl. CF6—1G 23
Grove Pl. La. CF6—1G 23
Grove Ter. CF6—1G 23
Grove, The. CF4—3E 13
Grove Way. CF3—4E 13
Guenever Clo. CF4—3B 4
Guildford Cres. CF1—4B 18
Guildford St. CF1—4B 18
Guildhall Pl. CF1—4A 18
Gwaun Clo. CF4—3E 9
Gwbert Clo. CF3—2G 13
Gwendoline Pl. CF2—4D 18
Gwendoline St. CF2—4D 18
Gwennyth St. CF2—6A 11
Gwent Rd. CF5—3A 16
Gwern Rhuddi Rd. CF2—5G 5
Gwynant Cres. CF2—2F 11
Gwyn James Ct. CF6—6C 20

Habershon St. CF2—4E 19
Hackerford Rd. CF2—5G 5
Hadfield Rd. CF1—6E 17
Hadley Ho. CF6—4F 23
Hafod St. CF1—5H 17
Haig Pl. CF5—6E 15
Halsbury Rd. CF5—2D 16
Halton Clo. CF6—5G 23
Hamilton St. CF1—3G 17
Hampton Ct. Rd. CF3—5A 12
Hampton Cres. CF4—4H 5
Hampton Cres. W. CF2—4G 5
Hampton Rd. CF4—3B 10
Hamstead Wlk. CF5—5D 14
Handel Clo. CF6—4F 23
Hannah Clo. CF4—1D 10
Hannah St. CF1—6B 18
Hanover Ct. CF4—1F 9
Hanover St. CF5—4E 17
Harbour View Rd. CF6—6E 21
Hardy Pl. CF2—2C 18
Harlech Dri. CF6—2C 22
Harlech Rd. CF3—4E 13
Harlequins Ct. CF2—1E 19
Harold St. CF2—2E 19
Harpur St. CF1—5A 18
Harriet St. CF2—1A 18
Harriet St. CF6—6D 20
Harris Av. CF3—3E 13
Harrismith Rd. CF2—6G 11
Harrowby La. CF1—2F 21
Harrowby Pl. CF1—2F 21
Harrowby St. CF1—1F 21
(in two parts)
Hartland Rd. CF3—2C 12
Harvey St. CF5—3E 17
Hastings Av. CF6—1E 23
Hastings Clo. CF6—1E 23
Hastings Pl. CF6—1E 23
Hatherleigh Rd. CF3—3C 12
Haul Fryn. CF4—5F 3
Havelock Pl. CF1—6H 17
Havelock St. CF1—4A 18
Haverford Way. CF5—5H 15
Hawfinch Clo. CF3—6H 5
Hawthorn Av. CF6—2E 23
Hawthorn Clo. CF6—3B 22
Hawthorn Rd. CF4—4F 9
Hawthorn Rd. W. CF4—4F 9
Hawthorns, The. CF2—6A 6
Hayes Bri. Rd. CF1—4A 18

Hayes, The. CF1—4A 18
Hazeldene Av. CF2—6A 11
Hazel Gro. CF6—3B 22
Hazelhurst Rd. CF4—4F 9
Hazel Pl. CF5—6D 8
Hazel Rd. CF6—3E 23
Hazel Tree Clo. CF4—1A 8
Hazelwood Dri. CF2—6G 7
Hazlitt Clo. CF3—5D 6
Heath Av. CF6—6B 20
Heathcliffe Clo. CF3—5F 7
Heather Av. CF5—3B 16
Heather Pl. CF5—1H 15
Heathfield Pl. CF4—5C 10
Heathfield Rd. CF4—5C 10
Heath Halt Rd. CF2—2E 11
Heath Pk. Av. CF4—2D 10
Heath Pk. Cres. CF4—3E 11
Heath Pk. La. CF4—4B 10 &
2E 11
Heath St. CF1—4G 17
Heath Way. CF4—2E 11
Heathwood Gro. CF4—3E 11
Heathwood Rd. CF4—3B 10
Heddfan N. CF2—6B 6
Heddfan S. CF2—6B 6
Hedel Rd. CF1—3C 16
Helen Pl. CF2—2D 18
Helen St. CF2—2D 18
Hendre Clo. CF5—1C 16
Hendre Gdns. CF5—1C 16
Hendre Rd. CF3—1F 13
Hendy St. CF2—6B 11
Hengoed Clo. CF5—5G 15
Henley Clo. CF5—6G 9
Henllys Rd. CF2—1F 11
Henry St. CF1—1F 21
Heol Aer. CF4—5A 4
Heol Aradur. CF5—4D 8
Heol Berry. CF4—2A 2
Heol Blakemore. CF4—2F 9
Heol Booker. CF4—2F 9
Heol Briwnant. CF4—4A 4
Heol Brynglas. CF4—5G 3
Heol Caerhys. CF4—6A 4
Heol Carnau. CF5—6H 15
Heol Carne. CF4—4H 9
Heol Cattwg. CF4—4H 9
Heol Cefn Ôn. CF4—2E 5
Heol Chappell. CF4—2F 9
Heol Coed Cae. CF4—4A 10
Heol Dennant. CF5—1A 16
Heol Derlwyn. CF4—5H 3
Heol Deva. CF5—6G 15
Heol Dolwen. CF4—3A 10
Heol Don. CF4—2F 9
Heol Dyfed. CF4—2B 10
Heol Ebwy. CF5—5H 15
Heol Eglwys. CF5—5A 16
Heol Erwin. CF4—4A 4
Heol Esgyn. CF2—1E 11
Heol Fair. CF5—6G 9
Heol Ffynnon Wen. CF4—5F 3
Heol Gabriel. CF4—4H 9
Heol Goch. CF4—2A 2
Heol Gwent. CF4—2B 10
Heol Gwilym. CF5—6D 8
Heol Gwrgan. CF4—2F 9
Heol Gwyndaf. CF4—6D 4
Heol Gwynedd. CF4—2B 10
Heol Harlech. CF5—1C 16
Heol Hendre. CF4—5A 4
Heol Hir. CF4—1C 4
Heol Iestyn. CF4—2H 9
Heol Ifor. CF4—2A 10
Heol Isaf. CF4—1B 8
(Radyr)
Heol Isaf. CF4—4H 3
(Rhiwbina)
Heol Iscoed. CF4—5A 4
Heol Las. CF3—3B 24
Heol Lewis. CF4—4A 4
Heol Llangan. CF4—1A 10
Heol Llanishen Fach. CF4—5H 3
Heol Mabon. CF4—5H 3
Heol Madoc. CF4—3A 10
Heol Mathew. CF4—2F 9
Heol Merlin. CF4—6D 4

Heol Muston. CF5—3H 15
Heol Nant Castan. CF4—4H 3
Heol Nest. CF4—2H 9
Heol Pantycelyn. CF4—6F 3
Heol Pantyderi. CF5—5G 15
Heol Pant-yr-yn. CF4—6F 3
Heol Pencarreg. CF4—5H 9
Heol Penlan. CF4—3E 9
Heol Pennar. CF5—5H 15
Heol Pentwyn. CF4—6F 3
Heol Penyfai. CF4—3A 10
Heol Powis. CF4—2B 10
Heol Poyston. CF5—6G 15
Heol Rhayader. CF4—3E 9
Heol Saint Denys. CF4—2E 5
Heol Seddon. CF5—5D 8
Heol Solva. CF5—5A 16
Heol Stradling. CF4—2H 9
Heol Syr Lewis. CF4—5B 2
Heol Trefgarne. CF5—6G 15
Heol Trelai. CF5—6F 15 to
5A 16
Heol Trenewydd. CF5—6G 15
Heol Ty'n-y-Cae. CF4—1H 9
Heol Ty'n-y-Coed. CF4—5A 4
Heol Uchaf. CF4—4H 3
Heol Urban. CF5—5E 9
Heol Waun-y-Nant. CF4—4H 9
Heol Wen. CF4—6H 3
Heol Wernlas. CF4—3A 10
Heol-y-Berllan. CF5—6G 15
Heol-y-Bont. CF4—6A 4
Heol-y-Bryn. CF4—6G 3
Heol-y-Castell. CF5—6G 15
Heol-y-cawl. CF6—2A 22
Heol-y-Coed. CF4—5G 3
Heol-y-Delyn. CF4—3F 5
Heol-y-Deri. CF4—5H 3
Heol-y-Felin. CF4—5A 4
Heol-y-Felin. CF5—3A 16
Heol-y-Fforest. CF4—3D 2
Heol-y-Forlan. CF4—1G 9
Heol-y-Frenhines. CF6—3A 22
Heol-y-Gaer. CF5—6G 15
Heol-y-Gors. CF4—4A 10
Heol-y-Nant. CF4—2A 2
(Taff's Well)
Heol-y-Nant. CF4—1H 9
(Whitchurch)
Heol-y-Parc. CF3—1C 6
Heol-y-Pavin. CF5—6F 9
Heol-yr-Ffail. CF4—6A 4
Heol-yr-Odyn. CF5—6F 15
Heol-yr-Ynys. CF4—3B 2
Heol-y-Waun. CF4—4H 9
Heol-y-Wenallt. CF4—1G 3
Heol y Wern. CF4—5A 4
Herbert March Clo. CF5—4D 8
Herbert St. CF1—5B 18
Herbert St. CF4—6C 10
Herbert Ter. CF6—6C 20
Hereford St. CF1—5G 17
Heritage Pk. CF3—5H 7
Herman Hill. CF4—4C 2
Heron Rd. CF3—4E 13
Hewell Ct. CF1—1D 20
Hewell St. CF6—6D 20
Hickman Rd. CF6—6D 20
Highbury Pl. CF5—5F 15
Highbury Rd. CF5—5G 15
High Croft Wlk. CF3—3D 12
Highfield Clo. CF6—1C 22
Highfield Rd. CF4 & CF2—3E 11
Highfields. CF5—5F 9
Highlands. CF3—5C 12
Highmead Rd. CF5—4G 15
High St. Cardiff, CF1—4A 18
High St. Llandaff, CF5—1C 16
High St. Penarth, CF6—1G 23
High St. Arc. CF1—4A 18
High View Rd. CF6—6D 20
Highwalls Av. CF6—1A 22
Highwalls End. CF6—1A 22
Highwalls Rd. CF6—2A 22
Hiles Rd. CF5—4G 15
Hillary Clo. CF4—4D 4
Hillcot Clo. CF4—3E 5
Hillrise. CF2—2H 11

Hillside Pk. Est. CF4—1A 2
Hill-snook Rd. CF5—4G 15
Hills St. CF1—4A 18
Hill St. CF6—6E 21
Hill Ter. CF6—6D 20
Hill View. CF5—1G 15
Hilton Pl. CF4—4F 9
Hinton St. CF2—4E 19
Hirst Cres. CF5—6D 8
Hirwain St. CF2—1H 17
Hodges Row. CF1—6B 18
Hodges Sq. CF1—6B 18
Hollybush Est. CF4—6E 3
Hollybush Rise. CF2—1H 11
Hollybush Rd. CF2—1G 11 to
1A 12
Hollycroft Clo. CF5—3A 16
Holly Gro. CF4—1E 5
Holly Rd. CF5—1H 15
Holly Ter. CF4—5G 9
Holmesdale Clo. CF1—2D 20
Holmesdale St. CF1—2D 20
Holmeside. CF4—2E 5
Holmsdale Pl. CF6—2H 23
Holmwood Clo. CF2—3G 11
Homelands Rd. CF4—1A 10
Honeysuckle Clo. CF5—1G 15
Honiton Rd. CF3—6E 7
Hope St. CF1—5B 18
(in two parts)
Housman Clo. CF3—5E 7
Howard Gdns. CF2—3C 18
Howard Pl. CF2—3C 18
Howard St. CF2—4D 18
Howard Ter. CF2—3C 18
Howell Rd. CF5—4G 15
Howell's Cres. CF5—1D 16
Hughs Clo. CF4—4E 9
Hunt Clo. CF4—4D 4
Hunters Ridge. CF2—3F 11
Hunter St. CF2—1F 21
Hurford Pl. CF2—5G 5
Hurman St. CF1—1F 21
Huron Cres. CF2—3F 11
Hydrangea Clo. CF2—6H 5

Iestynan Av. CF1—2F 17
Iestyn St. CF2—2F 17
Ilchester Rd. CF3—1E 13
Ilfracombe Cres. CF3—2E 13
Illtyd Rd. CF5—3F 15
Ilton Rd. CF2—6H 11
Inchmarnock St. CF2—4D 18
Inglefield Av. CF4—5D 10
Insole Clo. CF5—1B 16
Insole Gdns. CF5—1C 16
Insole Gro. E. CF5—1B 16
Insole Gro. W. CF5—1B 16
Insole Pl. CF5—2C 16
Instow Pl. CF3—1F 13
Inverness Pl. CF2—6B 11
Ipswich Rd. CF3—6A 12
Iron Bri. Rd. CF4—5C 2
Iron St. CF2—3D 18
Ivor St. CF1—4C 18
Ivydale. CF4—4 5
Ivy St. CF5—3D 16
Ivy St. CF6—1F 23

Jackson Rd. CF5—4F 15
Jacrow Sq. CF5—5G 15
James St. CF1—1F 21
Janet St. CF2—3D 18
Jasper Clo. CF5—5E 9
Jellicoe Gdns. CF2—2E 19
Jestyn Clo. CF6—1B 22
Jevan Clo. CF5—4D 8
John Morgan Clo. CF5—4E 9
Johns La. CF4—6G 9
Johnston Rd. CF4—4B 4
John St. CF1—5B 18
John St. CF6—6F 21
Jones Ct. CF1—4A 18
Joseph Parry Clo. CF6—5C 20
Jubilee La. CF6—1H 23
Jubilee St. CF1—5G 17
Jubilee Trading Est. CF1—4D 18
Junction Lock Rd. CF1—1H 21

Junction Ter. CF4—2C 8
Justin Clo. CF2—3G 11

Kames Pl. CF2—4C 18
Kane Clo. CF4—6D 4
Kelston Clo. CF4—2F 9
Kelston Pl. CF4—2F 9
Kelston Rd. CF4—2F 9
Kelvin Rd. CF2—6B 11
Kemys Pl. CF4—4A 10
Kenfig Rd. CF4—4B 10
Kenmuir Rd. CF2—2F 19
Kennerleigh Rd. CF3—3C 12
Kennilworth Ct. CF5—2B 16
Kennington Clo. CF4—3C 4
Kensington Av. CF5—3C 16
Kent St. CF1—1D 20
Kenwood Rd. CF5—4F 15
Kenyon Rd. CF2—2G 19
Keppoch St. CF2—1B 18
Kerrigan Clo. CF5—6D 8
Kerrycroy St. CF2—4D 18
Kestrel Clo. CF2—6H 5
Kestrel Way. CF6—5G 23
Keswick Av. CF2—4E 11
Kewstoke Av. CF3—2D 12
Kewstoke Clo. CF3—2D 12
Kewstoke Pl. CF3—2D 12
Keyes Av. CF2—2E 11
Keynsham Rd. CF4—3A 10
Keyston Rd. CF5—5D 8
Kilcatton St. CF2—4D 18
Kilgetty Clo. CF5—5G 15
Kilgetty Ct. CF5—1F 15
Kimberley Rd. CF4—5D 4
Kimberley Ter. CF4—5D 4
Kincraig St. CF2—1B 18
Kingarth St. CF2—4D 18
King Edward VII Av. CF1—2H 17
Kingfisher Clo. CF4—6H 7
King George V Dri. CF4—4D 10
King George V Dri. E. CF4
—4D 10
King George V Dri. N. CF4
—2D 10
King Groege V Dri. W. CF4
—4C 10
Kings Av. CF4—2C 8
Kingsland Rd. CF4—3F 9
Kingsland Rd. CF5—3D 16
Kings Rd. CF1—2F 17
Kings Rd. CF4—2C 8
Kingston Rd. CF1—4F 17
King St. CF4—2A 2
King St. CF6—6E 21
Kings Way. CF1—3A 18
King Wood Clo. CF3—5A 12
Kipling Clo. CF3—6D 6
Kipling Clo. CF6—6D 20
Kirkwall Ct. CF2—2F 19
Kitchener Rd. CF1—4F 17
Knightswell Rd. CF5—6E 15
Knowbury Av. CF6—5G 23
Knox Rd. CF2—3B 18
Kyle Av. CF4—2A 8
Kyle Cres. CF4—2A 10
Kymin Rd. CF6—1H 23
Kymin Ter. CF6—1H 23
Kyveilog St. CF1—2F 17

Laburnum Pl. CF5—1H 15
Laburnum Way. CF6—3B 22
(Dinas Powis)
Laburnum Way. CF6—2E 23
(Penarth)
Lady Margaret Ct. CF3—6H 11
Lady Margaret's Ter. CF2
—4D 18
Lady Mary Rd. CF2—5F 11
Ladysmith Rd. CF2—6H 11
Lake Rd. E. CF2—2F 11
Lake Rd. N. CF2—2E 11
Lake Rd. W. CF2—2E 11
Lakeside Dri. CF2—2F 11
Lakeview Clo. CF2—2F 11
Laleston Clo. CF5—5G 15
Lamby Way. CF3—1G 19

Langdale Clo. CF2—5G 11
Langland Rd. CF3—4E 13
Langport Av. CF3—1F 13
Lansdowne Av. E. CF1—4D 16
Lansdowne Av. W. CF1—4D 16
Lansdowne Rd. CF5—3D 16
Larch Ct. CF4—4D 2
Larch Gro. CF4—2F 5
Larkwood Av. CF6—3G 23
Laugharne Av. CF3—4E 13
Laugharne Rd. CF3—4E 13
Launcelot Cres. CF4—3B 4
Lauriston Pk. CF5—6G 15
Lavender Gro. CF5—1G 15
Lavernock Rd. CF6—3F to 6F 23
Lawrenny Av. CF1—5D 16
Laytonia Av. CF4—5C 10
Lead St. CF2—3D 18
Leamington Rd. CF4—1H 9
Leckwith Av. CF1—4E 17
Leckwith Clo. CF1—5F 17
Leckwith Industrial Est. CF1
—1B 20
Leckwith Pl. CF1—4F 17
Leckwith Rd. CF1—4A 20 to
4F 17
Lee Clo. CF3—3H 11
Lee Clo. CF6—1B 22
Leon Av. CF4—2A 2
Letterston Rd. CF3—3E 13
Lettons Way. CF6—1A 22
Letty St. CF2—1A 18
Leven Clo. CF2—2F 11
Lewis Rd. CF1—4D 18
Lewis Rd. CF6—4A 20
Lewis Rd. Industrial Est. CF1
—5D 18
Lewis St. CF1—4G 17
Library St. CF5—3F 17
Lilac Clo. CF5—6C 8
Lily St. CF2—2C 18
Limebourne Ct. CF4—4H 9
Lime Clo. CF4—3C 8
Lime Gro. CF5—6D 8
Limeslade Clo. CF5—2B 16
Limewood Clo. CF3—6G 7
Lincoln Ct. CF3—2H 11
Lincoln St. CF5—3D 16
Linden Av. CF2—6G 11
Linden Gro. CF3—3D 12
Lindway Ct. CF5—2D 16
Linnet Clo. CF4—6H 5
Lionel Rd. CF5—3D 16
Lisvane Rd. CF4—4E 5
Lisvane St. CF2—6D 10
Littlecroft Av. CF5—3B 16
Lit. Dock St. CF6—6D 20
Lit. Mill. CF4—4G 9
Lit. Orchard. CF6—2C 22
Littleton St. CF1—4F 17
Llanbedr Rd. CF5—2A 16
Llanbleddian Gdns. CF2—2A 18
Llanbradach St. CF1—4G 17
Llancaiach Rd. CF4—3H 9
Llandaff Clo. CF6—2E 23
Llandaff Pl. CF5—2E 17
Llandaff Rd. CF1—2E 17
Llandennis Av. CF2—1F 11
Llandennis Grn. CF2—1F 11
Llandennis Rd. CF2—1E 11
Llandetty Rd. CF5—2A 16
Llandilo Clo. CF6—2C 22
Llandinam Cres. CF4—6H 9
Llandough Hill. CF6—4B 20
Llandough St. CF2—2A 18
Llandough Trading Est. CF1
—3B 20
Llandovery Clo. CF5—5G 15
Llandow Rd. CF5—5H 15
Llandudno Rd. CF3—3E 13
Llandyfrig Clo. CF6—2C 22
Llanedeyrn Clo. CF3—4H 11
Llanedeyrn Dri. CF3—2A 12
Llanedeyrn Rd. CF3—5H 11
Llaneurwg Way. CF3—6G 7
Llanfair Rd. CF1—2E 17
Llangattock Rd. CF5—2A 16
Llangefni Pl. CF4—4C 4

Llangorse Rd. CF2—6G 5
Llangranog Pl. CF4—4B 4
Llangranog Rd. CF4—4B 4
Llangybi Clo. CF5—6D 14
Llangynidr Rd. CF5—2A 16
Llanidloes Rd. CF4—5H 9
Llanina Gro. CF3—2G 13
Llanishen Cl. CF4—5D 4
Llanishen St. CF4—5D 10
Llanmaes St. CF1—1D 20
Llanmorlais Rd. CF4—6A 10
Llanon Rd. CF4—4C 4
Llanover Rd. CF5—6D 14
Llanrumney Av. CF3—3D 12
Llansdowne Av. CF4—1A 10
Llanstephan Rd. CF3—4E 13
Llanstarnam Rd. CF4—5H 9
Llantrisant Rd. CF5—3A 8 to
6F 9
Llantrisant St. CF2—1H 17
Llantwit St. CF2—2B 18
Llanwern Rd. CF5—4G 15
Llewellyn Av. CF5—3F 15
Lloyd Av. CF5—2B 16
Llwyd Coed. CF4—4F 3
Llwyn Bryn Melyn. CF4—1A 8
Llwyn Castan. CF2—6A 6
Llwyn Drysgol. CF4—1A 8
Llwyn Grug. CF4—5A 4
Llwyn Onn. CF4—4G 3
Llwyn Rhosyn. CF4—5A 4
Llwynfedw Gdns. CF4—2B 10
Llwynfedw Rd. CF4—2A 10
Llwyn-y-grant Pl. CF3—5H 11
Llwyn-y-grant Rd. CF3—5H 11
Llwyn-y-grant Ter. CF3—5H 11
Llwyn-y-pia Rd. CF4—2F 5
Llyn Clo. CF2—2F 11
Llys Tal-y-Bont. CF4—6B 10
Llys Tal-y-Bont Rd. CF4—6C 10
Llyswen Rd. CF2—1F 11
Lochaber St. CF2—6G 11
Locks Rd. CF1—3G to 2G 21
Lodge Clo. CF4—1E 5
Loftus St. CF5—3D 16
Lomond Cres. CF2—2G 11
Loncae Porth. CF4—4A 4
Lon Fach. CF4—6H 3
Lon Ganol. CF4—6H 3
Longcross St. CF2—3C 18
Longhouse Clo. CF4—3E 5
Longleat Clo. CF4—3F 5
Longmeadow Dri. CF6—3B 22
Longreach Clo. CF5—5D 14
Longships Rd. CF1—3H 21
Longspears Av. CF4—4A 10
Long Wood Dri. CF4—6C 2
Lon Isa. CF4—6H 3
Lon Madoc. CF4—3A 10
Lon Owain. CF5—6F 15
Lon Penllyn. CF4—1H 9
Lonsdale Rd. CF3—4A 12
Lon Ty'n-y-cae. CF4—1A 10
Lon Ucha. CF4—6H 3
Lon Werdd Clo. CF5—4E 15
Lon-y-Castell. CF5—6G 15
Lon-y-Celyn. CF4—1F 9
Lon-y-dail. CF4—6H 3
Lon-y-dderwen. CF4—6H 3
Lon-y-deri. CF4—6H 3
Lon-y-ffin. CF4—5E 15
Lon-y-groes. CF4—3B 10
Lon-y-mynydd. CF4—6A 4
Lon-y-nant. CF4—6A 4
Lon-y-parc. CF4—2H 9
Lon-yr-Efail. CF5—6F 15
Lon-y-rhyd. CF4—6H 3
Lon Ysgubor. CF4—5H 3
Lon-y-winci. CF4—5H 3
Lord St. CF6—6F 21
Lothian Cres. CF3—4H 11
Loudoun Sq. CF1—6B 18
Louisa Pl. CF1—1F 21
Love La. CF1—4B 18
Lwr. Acre. CF5—6F 15
Lwr. Cathedral Rd. CF1—4H 17
Lowther Rd. CF2—2B 18
Lowther Rd. CF2—2B 18

Lucas St. CF2—6A 11
Lucknow St. CF1—6G 17
Ludlow Clo. CF1—1E 21
Ludlow La. CF6—1G 23
Ludlow St. CF1—1D 20
Ludlow St. CF6—1G 23
Lundy Clo. CF4—5C 4
Lydford Clo. CF4—1H 9
Lydstep Cres. CF4—6H 9
Lydstep Flats. CF4—5H 9
Lynch Blosse Clo. CF5—5E 9
Lyncroft Clo. CF3—5F 7
Lyndhurst St. CF1—4F 17
Lynmouth Cres. CF3—4C 12
Lynton Clo. CF3—3D 12
Lynton Pl. CF3—3C 12
Lynton Ter. CF3—3C 12
Lynwood Ct. CF2—2C 18
Lyon Clo. CF1—2B 20

Macauley Av. CF3—6D 6
McCale Av. CF5—2A 16
Macdonald Clo. CF5—5E 15
Macdonald Pl. CF5—5E 15
Macdonald Rd. CF5—5E 15
Machen Clo. CF3—4A 24
Machen Pl. CF1—4G 17
Machen St. CF1—6G 17
Machen St. CF6—1F 23
Mackintosh Pl. CF2—6B 11
Madoc Clo. CF6—2C 22
Madoc Rd. CF2—3F 19
Maelfa. CF3—3A 12
Maelog Pl. CF4—6C 10
Maelog Rd. CF4—3A 10
Maes Glas. CF4—4G 9
Maes-y-Bryn. CF4—6B 2
Maes-y-bryn Rd. CF3—1C 6
Maes-y-Coed. CF4—6H 3
Maes-y-Coed Rd. CF4—1B 10
Maes-y-deri. CF4—6H 3
Maes-y-Felin. CF4—1H 9
Maes y Parc. CF4—1H 9
Maes yr Awel. CF4—1B 8
Maes yr haf. CF4—5F 3
Mafeking Rd. CF2—6G 11
Magnolia Clo. CF2—6H 5
Maindy Rd. CF2—6C 10
Main Rd. CF4—2A 2
Maitland Pl. CF1—6G 17
Maitland St. CF4—5C 10
Major Rd. CF5—4F 17
Maldwyn St. CF1—2F 17
Malefant St. CF2—6A 11
Mallard Clo. CF3—6G 7
Mallard Way. CF6—6G 23
Malmesmead Rd. CF3—6E 7
Malpas Clo. CF3—6H 7
Malvern Dri. CF4—6C 4
Mandeville Pl. CF1—4G 17
Mandeville St. CF1—4G 17
Manitoba Clo. CF2—2G 11
Manod Rd. CF4—5G 9
Manorbier Clo. CF6—2C 22
Manorbier Cres. CF3—3E 13
Manor Clo. CF4—2H 9
Manor Rise. CF4—3A 10
Manor St. CF4—5D 10
Manor Way. CF4—2A 10
Mansell Av. CF5—6D 14
Mansfield St. CF1—4G 17
Maple Bds. CF5—6B 8
Maple Rd. CF6—2E 23
Maple Tree Clo. CF4—1A 8
Maplewood Av. CF4—4F 9
Marchwood Clo. CF3—2E 13
Marcross Rd. CF5—5E 15
Mardy Rd. CF6F 13
Mardy St. CF1—5H 17
Margam Rd. CF4—5B 10
Maria St. CF1—5B 18
Marine Pde. CF6—3H 23
Marion Ct. CF4—4E 5
Marion St. CF2—3E 19
Marionville Gdns. CF5—1A 16
Maritime Rd. CF1—1G 21
Market Pl. CF5—3E 17
Market Rd. CF5—3E 17

Market St. CF4—4C 2
Mark St. CF1—4H 17
Marlborough Rd. CF2—6G 11
Marloes Rd. CF5—4F 15
Marshall Clo. CF5—2F 9
Marsham Ct. CF4—2C 8
Marshfield Rd. CF3—1C 24
Mary Ann St. CF1—4B 18
Maryport Rd. CF2—5F 11
Mary St. CF4—5F 9
Masefield Rd. CF6—1E 23
Mathew Wlk. CF5—5D 8
Maughan La. CF6—6F 21
Maughan Ter. CF6—6F 21
Maureen Av. CF5—3H 15
Mavis Gro. CF4—1B 10
Maxwell Rd. CF3—3E 13
Mayfair Dri. CF4—2C 4
Mayfield Av. CF5—1A 16
Mayflower Av. CF4—4B 4
Maynard Ct. CF5—1C 16
May St. CF2—6A 11
Meadow Clo. CF2—5H 5
Meadow La. CF6—4F 23
Meadowlark Clo. CF3—6G 7
Meadow St. CF1—2F 17
Meadvale Rd. CF3—1F 13
Melbourne La. CF4—5D 4
Melbourne Rd. CF4—5D 4
Meliden La. CF6—2F 23
Meliden Rd. CF6—2F 23
Melrose Av. CF3—6H 11
Melrose Clo. CF4—6H 3
Melville Av. CF3—5G 7
Menai Way. CF3—1F 13
Mendip Rd. CF3—2C 12
Merches Gdns. CF1—5H 17
Merches Pl. CF1—5H 17
Mercia Rd. CF2—3F 19
Meredith Rd. CF2—3F 19
Merlin Clo. CF3—3C 4
Merlin Clo. CF6—5G 23
Merthyr Rd. CF4—4C 2
(Tongwynlais)
Merthyr Rd. CF4—3H 9 & 3B 10
(Whitchurch)
Merthyr St. CF2—1H 17
Mervyn Rd. CF2—3F 19
Mervyn Rd. CF4—3H 9
Metal St. CF2—3D 18
Meteor St. CF2—3D 18
Meyrick Rd. CF5—5E 15
Michaelston Rd. CF5—6D 14
Mile Rd. CF6—4D 22
Millbrook Clo. CF6—1B 22
Millbrook Heights. CF6—1B 22
Millbrook Pk. CF4—2E 5
Millbrook Rd. CF6—1B 22
Mill Clo. CF4—4E 5
Mill Clo. CF6—2A 22
Mill Gdns. CF4—2E 5
Millfield. CF4—2E 5
Millfield Clo. CF3—1G 13
Millgate. CF4—4E 5
Millicent St. CF1—4B 18
Mill La. CF1—4A 18
Mill La. CF3—5D 6
(in two parts)
Mill La. CF5—1D 16
Mill Pl. CF4—2F 5
Mill Pl. CF5—3A 16
Millrace Clo. CF4—3E 5
Mill Rd. CF4—4E 5
(Llanishen)
Mill Rd. CF4—4C 2
(Tongwynlais)
Mill Rd. CF6—2A 22
Millwood. CF4—3E 5
Milton Pl. CF5—1A 16
Milton Rd. CF6—1F 23
Milton St. CF2—2C 18
Milverton Rd. CF3—6E 7
Minafon. CF4—4H 3
Minavon. CF4—2H 9
Minehead Rd. CF3—1E 13
Minister St. CF2—1A 18

Minney St. CF2—1A 18
(in two parts)
Minster Rd. CF2—1E 19
Min-y-Coed. CF4—6B 2
Min-y-Nant. CF4—6H 3
Miskin St. CF2—2A 18
Miterdale Clo. CF2—4F 11
Mitre Pl. CF5—6G 9
Moira Pl. CF2—3C 18
Moira St. CF2—3C 18
Moira Ter. CF2—3C 18
Mona Pl. CF2—2F 19
Monkstone Clo. CF6—4E 23
Monkstone Rise. CF3—2E 13
Monmouth St. CF1—5H 17
Montgomery St. CF2—6G 11
Monthermer Rd. CF2—6A 11
Moon St. CF2—3D 18
Moordale Rd. CF1—1E 21
Moore Clo. CF5—4F 15
Moore Rd. CF5—4F 15
Moorland Rd. CF2—2E to 4F 19
Moors La. CF1—4C 16
Morfa Cres. CF3—2G 13
Morgan Arc. CF1—4A 18
Morgan St. CF1—4B 18
Morlais St. CF2—6B 11
Morris Av. CF4—4B 4
Morris Finer Clo. CF5—4A 16
Mortimer Rd. CF1—2F 17
Mostyn Rd. CF5—5E 15
Mountbatten Clo. CF2—2E 11
Mountjoy Av. CF6—1E 23
Mountjoy Clo. CF6—1F 23
Mountjoy Cres. CF6—1E 23
Mountjoy La. CF2—1E 23
Mountjoy Pl. CF6—1E 23
Mt. Pleasant Av. CF3—1E 13
Mt. Pleasant La. CF3—1E 13
Mount Rd. CF6—2A 22
Mt. Stuart Sq. CF1—1F 21
Mount, The. CF6—2A 22
Moy Rd. CF2—1B 18
Moy Rd. CF4—1A 2
Muirton Rd. CF2—3F 19
Mullins Av. CF3—2F 13
Mundy Pl. CF2—1A 18
Murch Cres. CF6—2C 22
Murch Rd. CF6—2B 22
Murgwyn. CF4—5A 4
Murrayfield Rd. CF4—2B 10
Murray Wlk. CF1—4F 17
Museum Av. CF1—2A 18
Museum Pl. CF1—2A 18
Mylo Griffiths Clo. CF5—4E 9
Mynachdy Rd. CF4—5A & 5B 10
Myrtle Clo. CF6—2E 23

Nant Fawr Clo. CF2—1F 11
Nant Fawr Cres. CF2—1F 11
Nant Fawr Rd. CF2—1F 11
Nant yr Arthur. CF5—5D 14
Narberth Rd. CF5—5H 15
Neath St. CF2—4E 19
Nesta Rd. CF3—5D 16
Neville Pl. CF1—4G 17
Neville St. CF1—4G 17
Nevin Cres. CF3—3E 13
Newborough Av. CF5—5C 4
Newfoundland Rd. CF4—5C 10
Newgale Pl. CF5—5H 15
Newlands Ct. CF4—4E 5
Newminster Rd. CF2—1E 19
Newport Rd CF2 & CF3—3B 18
to 2A 24
Newport Rd. La. CF2—3C 18
Newport St. CF1—1E 21
New Rd. CF3—5C 12
Newton Rd. CF1—5F 17
Newton Rd. CF3—5G 13
New Zealand Rd. CF4—6C 10
Neyland Pl. CF5—5H 15
Nicholson Webb Clo. CF5—4D 8
Nigel Rowberry Clo. CF4—2D 4
Nightingale Pl. CF6—3C 22
Ninian Pk. Rd. CF1—4F 17
Ninian Rd. CF2—5F 11
Nora St. CF2—2D 18

Norbury Av. CF5—2A 16
Norbury Rd. CF4—2B 16
Norbury Rd. CF5—2A 16
Norfolk St. CF5—3D 16
Norman Rd. CF4—3F 9
Norman St. CF2—1B 18
Norris Clo. CF6—6B 20
Northam Av. CF3—2C 12
N. Church St. CF1—5B 18
Northcliffe. CF6—6F 21
Northcliffe Dri. CF6—6F 21
N. Clive St. CF1—6G 17
Northcote La. CF2—2B 18
Northcote St. CF2—2B 18
N. Edward St. CF1—3B 18
Northern Av. CF4—5E 3 to
3B 10
Northlands. CF3—5D 12
N. Luton Pl. CF2—4C 18
N. Morgan St. CF1—4G 17
N. Park Rd. CF2—3E 19
North Rise. CF4—4E 5
North Rd. CF4 & CF1—4B 10 to
3A 18
North St. CF1—6H 17
Northumberland St. CF5—4E 17
North View. CF4—1B 2
Norton Av. CF4—3B 10
Norwich Rd. CF3—6B 12
Nottage Rd. CF5—5G 15
Nottingham St. CF5—3D 16
Nursery Cotts. CF6—3A 22

Oak Ct. CF4—3D 2
Oakdene Clo. CF3—3G 11
Oakfield St. CF2—2C 18
Oaklands Clo. CF3—6G 7
Oakley Pl. CF1—1D 20
Oak Tree Clo. CF4—1A 8
Oakway. CF5—2G 15
Oak Wood Av. CF3—5A 12
Oakwood Clo. CF6—5C 20
Odet Ct. CF4—6E 3
Ogmore Rd. CF5—5G 15
Ogwen Dri. CF2—1F 11
Okehampton Av. CF3—5E 7
Old Church Rd. CF4—2G 9
Old Farm M. CF6—2A 22
Oldhill. CF3—1F 13
Old Malthouse. CF6—2A 22
Old Mill Rd. CF4—3E 5
Old Newport Rd. CF3—5H 7
Old Radyr Rd. CF4—4F 9
Old Vicarage Clo. CF4—5D 4
Ollivant Clo. CF5—4D 8
Ontario Way. CF2—2G 11
Orange Gro. CF5—6C 8
Orbit St. CF2—4C 18
Orchard Castle. CF4—3C 4
Orchard Clo. CF3—3D 24
Orchard Cres. CF6—2B 22
Orchard Dri. CF2—6G 9
Orchard Gro. CF4—5B 2
Orchard Pl. CF3—6G 7
Orchard Pl. CF1—3F 17
Orchard Rise. CF6—1E 23
Ordell St. CF2—3C 18
Orion Ct. CF2—3C 18
Ormonde Clo. CF3—4A 12
Osprey Clo. CF3—5G 7
Osprey Clo. CF6—6G 23
Oswestry Clo. CF3—4E 13
Othery Pl. CF3—5E 7
Oval, The. CF2—4G 11
Ovington Ter. CF5—2D 16
Owain Clo. CF2—3G 11
Owen's Ct. CF4—3B 10
Oxford Arc. CF1—4A 18
Oxford La. CF2—3C 18
Oxford St. CF2—2C 18
Oxwich Clo. CF5—2B 16

Pace Clo. CF5—5D 8
Padarn Clo. CF2—2F 11
Paddocks, The. CF6—4G 23
Paddock, The. CF2—5G 11
Paget Pl. CF5—6F 21
Paget Rd. CF6—6E 21

Paget St. CF1—6H 17
Paget Ter. CF6—6F 21
Palace Av. CF5—1D 16
Palace Rd. CF5—1D 16
Pantbach Av. CF4—3B 10
Pantbach Pl. CF4—3B 10
Pantbach Rd. CF4—1A 10
Panteg Clo. CF5—6D 14
Pant Glas. CF2—6C 6
Pantgwynlais. CF4—4D 2
Pantmawr Rd. CF4—6F 3
Pant Tawel La. CF4—1A 8
Pantycelyn Rd. CF6—5B 20
Pant-y-deri Clo. CF5—5G 15
Paper Mill Rd. CF1—3C 16
Parade, The. CF2—3C 18
Parade, The. CF4—3F 9
Parade, The. CF6—2C 22
Parc-y-Ty-Glas. CF4—6C 4
Park Av. CF4—1F 9
Park Cres. CF4—1F 9
Park End La. CF2—1E 11
Parker Pl. CF5—5F 15
Parker Rd. CF5—5F 15
Parkfield Pl. CF4—6C 10
Park Gro. CF1—2B 18
Park La. CF1—2A 18
Park La. CF4—1A 2
(Taff's Well)
Park La. CF4—1F 9
(Whitchurch)
Park Pl. CF1—2A 18
Park Rd. CF4—1B 8
(Radyr)
Park Rd. CF4—1F 9
(Whitchurch)
Park Rd. CF6—1A 22
(Dinas Powis)
Park Rd. CF6—2H 23
(Penarth)
Parkstone Av. CF3—5G 7
Park St. CF1—4A 18
Park View Ct. CF4—1F 9
Parkwall Rd. CF3—4E 13
Parracombe Clo. CF3—6E 7
Parracombe Cres. CF3—1D 12
Partridge Rd. CF2—2C 18
Patchway Cres. CF3—3C 12
Patterdale Clo. CF2—5F 11
Peach Pl. CF5—1H 15
Pearl Pl. CF2—3D 18
Pearl St. CF2—3D 18
Pearson St. CF2—2C 18
Pedair Erw Rd. CF4—2B 10
Pellett St. CF1—4B 18
Pembroke Rd. CF5—3E 17
Pembroke Ter. CF6—6F 21
Penally Rd. CF5—1A 16
Penarth Head La. CF6—1H 26
Penarth Rd. CF6 & CF1—5C 20
to 5A 18
Penbury Ct. CF4—5B 2
Pencader Rd. CF5—3A 16
Pencisely Av. CF5—2C 16
Pencisely Cres. CF5—2C 16
Pencisely Rise. CF5—2C 16
Pencisely Rd. CF5—2C 16
Pendine Rd. CF5—4A 16
Pendoylan Ct. CF5—3A 16
Pendragon Clo. CF4—3B 4
Pendraw Pl. CF2—1F 11
Pendwyallt Rd. CF4—6E 3
Pendyris St. CF1—5H 17
Penedre. CF5—6G 9
Penford Ct. CF2—2B 18
Pengam Rd. CF2—1F 19
Pengwern Rd. CF5—3A 16
Penhevad St. CF1—1D 20
Penhill Clo. CF5—2E 17
Penhill St. CF5—2E 17
Pen-hill Rd. CF1—2E 17
Penlan Rise. CF6—5B 20
Penlan Rd. CF6—4B 20
Penlline Ct. CF4—2G 9
Penlline Rd. CF4—2G 9
Penlline St. CF2—2B 18
Penllyn Rd. CF5—4F 17
Penmaen Wlk. CF5—6D 14

Penmark Grn. CF5—4E 15
Penmark Rd. CF5—5E 15
Pennant Cres. CF2—1G 11
Pennard Pl. CF4—4B 10
Pennine Clo. CF4—6C 4
Pennsylvania. CF3—2H & 3H 11
Penrhos. CF4—6A 2
Penrhos Cres. CF3—3E 13
Penrhyn Clo. CF3—2G 13
Pensarn Rd. CF3—2G 13
Pent Lee. CF2—6A 6
Pentrebane Rd. CF5—6A 8
Pentrebane St. CF1—1D 20
Pentre Gdns. CF1—5H 17
Pentre Pl. CF1—6H 17
Pentre St. CF1—6H 17
Pentwyn. CF4—6A 2
Pentwyn Dri. CF2—1A 12
Pentwyn Rd. CF2—4H 5 to 6C 6
Pentwyn Shopping Centre.
CF2—6B 6
Pentyrch St. CF2—1H 17
Pen-y-bryn Pl. CF4—5C 10
Pen-y-bryn Rd. CF2—6G 5
Pen-y-bryn Rd. CF4—5C 10
Pen-y-bryn Way. CF4—5C 10
Pen-y-Cefn. CF4—3B 4
Penycraig. CF4—4H 3
Pen-y-dre. CF4—1G 9
Penygarn Rd. CF5—3H 15
Pen-y-groes Av. CF4—6B 4
Pen-y-groes Rd. CF4—6B 4
Penylan Ct. CF2—4G 11
Pen-y-lan Pl. CF2—6B 11
Pen-y-lan Rd. CF2—6B 11
Pen-y-lan Ter. CF3—5H 11
Pen-y-peel Rd. CF5—3E 17
Pen-y-turnpike Rd. CF6—1A 22
Pen-y-wain La. CF2—6B 11
Pen-y-wain Pl. CF2—6B 11
Pen-y-wain Rd. CF2—6B 11
Pen-y-waun. CF6—2B 22
Pepys Cres. CF3—1D 12
Percival Clo. CF4—3B 4
Perclose. CF6—2B 22
Percy St. CF1—5A 18
Perrots Clo. CF5—1A 16
Perry St. CF3—3E 17
Petherton Pl. CF3—1E 13
Pethybridge Rd. CF5—3F 15
Petrel Clo. CF6—5G 23
Philip Clo. CF4—1B 10
Philip St. CF1—4F 17
Philog, The. CF4—3A 10
Pickwick Clo. CF4—3D 4
Picton Pl. CF1—4F 17
Picton Way. CF1—4F 17
Piercefield Pl. CF2—3D 18
Pill St. CF6—6C 20
Pilton Pl. CF4—5B 10
Pine Ct. CF4—3D 2
Pinehurst Rd. CF5—1G 15
Pine Tree Clo. CF4—6A 2
Pinewood Clo. CF6—5C 20
Pine Wood Cres. CF3—4A 12
Piper Clo. CF5—5D 8
Pitman La. CF1—3G 17
Pitman St. CF1—3G 17
Planet St. CF2—3C 18
Plantagenet St. CF1—4H 17
Plas Essyllt. CF6—3B 22
Plas-mawr Rd. CF5—6D 8
Plas Newydd. CF4—3H 9
Plasnewydd Pl. CF2—1C 18
Plasnewydd Rd. CF2—1B &
2C 18
Plasnewydd Sq. CF2—1B 18
Plassey Sq. CF6—6E 21
Plassey St. CF6—6E 21
Plas Treoda. CF4—3H 9
Plasturton Av. CF2—1F 17
Plasturton Gdns. CF1—3G 17
Plasturton Pl. CF1—3G 17
Plas-y-Delyn. CF4—3F 5
Plas-y-llan. CF4—3H 9
Platinum St. CF2—3D 18
Plover Way. CF6—5G 23
Plymouth Rd. CF6—4G to 2G 23

Plymouth St. CF1—3A 18
Plymouth Wood Clo. CF5
—3H 15
Plymouth Wood Cres. CF5
—3G 15
Plymouth Wood Rd. CF5
—3H 15
Pomergelli Rd. CF4—3F 9
Pomeroy St. CF1—2F 21
Pontcanna Pl. CF1—2F 17
Pontcanna St. CF1—2F 17
Pontfaen. CF2—5H 5
Pontrilas Clo. CF5—6D 14
Poplar Clo. CF5—6C 8
Poplar Rd. CF5—6C 8
Poppyfield Clo. CF3—1G 13
Porlock Rd. CF3—6F 7
Portfield Cres. CF4—6D 4
Porthamal Gdns. CF4—1A 10
Porthamal Rd. CF4—1A 10
Porthcawl Rd. CF5—5G 15
Porthkerry Pl. CF4—5B 10
Portland Clo. CF6—3H 23
Portland Pl. CF4—3F 9
Port Madoc Rd. CF3—2G 13
Portmanmoor Rd. CF2—4E &
5E 19
Portmanmoor Rd. Industrial Est.
CF2—5E 19
Port Rd. CF5—6D 14
Powys CLo. CF6—1C 22
Powys Dri. CF6—1B 22
Powys Gdns. CF6—1C 22
Powys Pl. CF6—1C 22
Powys Rd. CF6—3F 23
Prendergast Pl. CF5—6H 15
Prestatyn Rd. CF3—2F 13
Preswylfa. CF5—2D 16
Priest Rd. CF2—2D 18
Primrose Clo. CF3—5D 12
Prince Leopold St. CF2—4D 18
Princes Av. CF2—2D 18
Princes Ct. CF2—3B 18
Princes St. CF2—3D 18
Pritchard Clo. CF5—5E 9
Prospect Dri. CF5—1B 16
Pum Erw Rd. CF4—2B 10
Purbeck St. CF5—3E 17
Purcell Rd. CF3—6F 7
Purcell Rd. CF4—6F 23
Pwllheli Cl. CF3—6F 7
Pwll mawr Av. CF3—4E 13
Pwllmelin La. CF5—1B 16
Pwll Melin Rd. CF5—6D 8
Pyle Rd. CF5—6G 15

Quarry Clo. CF5—1G 15
Quarry Cres. CF5—1G 15
Quarry Dale. CF3—5D 12
Quarry Ho. CF1—4C 18
Quarry Rd. CF5—4E 9
Quay St. CF1—4A 18
Queen Ann Sq. CF1—2H 17
Queensbury Rd. CF3—4A 12
Queens Rd. CF6—6E 21
Queen St. CF3—3A 18
Queen St. CF4—4C 2
Queen St. Arc. CF1—4A 18
Queenwood. CF3—4A 12
Queen Wood Clo. CF3—4G 11
Quentin St. CF4—5C 10

Radnor Ct. CF5—3E 17
Radnor Rd. CF5—3E 17
Radyr Ct. Clo. CF5—5F 9
Radyr Ct. Rise. CF5—5F 9
Radyr Ct. Rd. CF5—4E & 5F 9
Radyr Farm Rd. CF4—3C 8
Radyr Pl. CF4—5B 10
Raglan CLo. CF3—4A 24
Raglan Clo. CF2—3D 18
Railway St. CF2—3D 18
Railway Ter. CF1—4F 17
Railway Ter. CF4—4C 2
Railway Ter. CF6—6B 20
(Cogan)
Railway Ter. CF6—1G 23
(Penarth)

30

Raisdale Rd. CF6—3G 23
Rannoch Dri. CF2—2G 11
Ravensbrook. CF4—5B 2
Ravens Ct. Clo. CF3—5H 11
Raven Way. CF2—6G 23
Rawden Pl. CF1—4G 17
Rectory Ct. CF4—2E 5
Rectory Rd. CF1—3E 17
Rectory Rd. CF6—1H 26
Rectory Rd. La. CF6—1H 23
Redbrink Ct. CF5—3G 15
Redcliffe Av. CF5—3C 16
Red Ho. Clo. CF5—3H 15
Red Ho. Cres. CF5—4G 15
Red Ho. Pl. CF5—3H 15
Red Ho. Rd. CF5—3G 15
Redlands Av. CF6—1E 23
Redlands Ho. CF6—1E 23
Redlands Rd. CF6—6B 20
Redlaver St. CF1—6H 17
Redwood Clo. CF6 7
Regina Ter. CF5—2D 16
Reigate Clo. CF4—2C 4
Relf Rd. CF3—3E 13
Rennie St. CF1—4G 17
Restways Clo. CF4—5D 8
Retreat, The. CF2—5H 11
Rheidol Clo. CF4—5E 5
Rhigoes Gdns. CF2—6D 10
Rhigoes St. CF2—6D 10
Rhiwbina Hill. CF4—1E to 5G 3
Rhiwderyn Clo. CF5—6D 14
Rhiwlas. CF4—3A 4
Rhiw Ddar. CF4—1A 2
Rhiwr Ddar Ho. CF4—1A 2
Rhododendron Clo. CF2—6H 5
Rhosllan. CF4—5A 4
Rhossilly Av. CF3—3E 13
Rhossilly Rd. CF3—3E 13
Rhuddlan Way. CF6—1C 22
Rhydhelig Av. CF4—3B 10
Rhyd-y-penau Clo. CF4—1E 11
Rhyd-y-penau Rd. CF2—1E 11
Rhyl Rd. CF3—3E 13
Rhymney River Bri. Rd. CF3
—6B 12
Rhymney St. CF2—1B 18
Rhymney Ter. CF2—1A 18
Richard Lewis Clo. CF5—5E 9
Richards St. CF2—1A 18
Richards Ter. CF2—2D 18
Richmond Cres. CF2—2B 18
Richmond Rd. CF2—1B 18
Rich's Rd. CF4—3B 10
Ridgeway. CF4—2E 5
Ridgeway Rd. CF3—2C 12
Risca Clo. CF3—6H 7
Rise, The. CF4—5E 5
Riverdale. CF5—3H 15
Riverdale. CF5—4E 9
Riverside Ter. CF5—3B 16
River View. CF4—5G & 6H 9
River View Ct. CF5—4F 15
Roath Ct. Pl. CF2—1D 18
Roath Ct. Rd. CF2—1D 18
Roath Dock Rd. CF1—1H 21
Robert St. CF2—6A 11
Robert St. CF2—3B 16
Robin Clo. CF2—6H 5
Robin Hill. CF6—3B 16
Robinswood Clo. CF6—3G 23
Robinswood Cres. CF6—3G 23
Roche Cres. CF5—6C 8
Rockrose Way. CF6—6C 20
Rockwood Rd. CF4—1B 2
Rogersmoor Clo. CF6—3F 23
Rogerstone Clo. CF3—6H 7
Rolls St. CF1—4F 17
Romilly Cres. CF1—3E 17
Romilly Pl. CF5—3E 17
Romilly Rd. CF5—3E 17
Romilly Rd. W. CF5—2D 16
Romney Wlk. CF6—6D 20
Rompney Ter. CF3—5D 12
Ronald Pl. CF5—3H 15
Rookwood Av. CF6—5F 9
Rookwood Clo. CF5—6F 9
Rookwood St. CF1—6G 17

Roseberry Pl. CF6—2F 23
Rosedale Clo. CF5—1G 15
Rosemount Pl. CF4—4B 10
Rose St. CF2—2C 18
Rosewood Clo. CF4—2E 5
Rosset Clo. CF3—1G 13
Round Wood. CF3—2A 12
Round Wood Clo. CF3—4A 12
Rover Way. CF2—1F to 6F 19
Rover Way Industrial Est. CF2
—1F 19
Rowan Clo. CF6—4G 23
Rowan St. CF5—1C 16
Rowan Way. CF4—2F 5
Roxburgh Garden Ct. CF6
—2H 23
Royal Arc. CF1—4A 18
Royal Clo. CF6—6E 21
Royal Stuart La. CF1—1F 21
Ruby St. CF2—3D 18
Rudry Rd. CF4—2G 5
Rudry St. CF1—6G 17
Rudry St. CF6—1F 23
Runcorn Clo. CF4—3E 9
Rushbrook Clo. CF4—3E 9
Ruskin Clo. CF3—6D 6
Russell St. CF2—2B 18
Ruthin Gdns. CF2—2A 18
Rutland St. CF1—5G 17
Ryder St. CF1—3G 17

Sachville Av. CF4—5C 10
St Agatha Rd. CF4—3C 10
St Agnes Rd. CF4—3B 10
St Aidan Cres. CF4—3B 10
St Alban's Av. CF4—3B 10
St Ambrose Clo. CF4—3A 22
St Ambrose Rd. CF4—3C 10
St Andrew's Cres. CF1—3B 18
St Andrew's La. CF1—3B 18
St Andrew's Pl. CF1—3A 18
St Angela Rd. CF4—4C 10
St Anne's Av. CF6—3F 23
St Anthony Rd. CF4—3C 10
St Asaph Clo. CF4—1C 10
St Augustine Rd. CF4—3C 10
St Augustine's Cres. CF6—6F 21
St Augustine's Path. CF1
—6F 21
St Augustine's Pl. CF6—6F 21
St Augustine's Rd. CF6—6F 21
St Baruch Clo. CF3 A 22
St Benedict Cres. CF4—3C 10
St Brigid Rd. CF4—1C 10
St Brioc Rd. CF4—1C 10
St Cadoc Rd. CF4—2C 10
St Cadoc's Av. CF6—3A 22
St Cenydd Rd. CF4—1D 10
St Clement's Ct. CF2—5A 6
St Cyres Clo. CF6—1E 23
St Cyres Rd. CF6—1E 23
St David Av. CF6—1B 22
St David's Centre. CF1—4A 18
St David's Cres. CF5—4H 15
St David's Cres. CF6—2D 22
St David's Hall. CF1—4A 18
St David's Rd. CF4—3H 9
St David's Way. CF1—4A 18
St Denis Rd. CF4—2D 10
St Dogmael's Av. CF4—6D 10
St Donat's Clo. CF6—2B 22
St Donat's Rd. CF1—5F 17
St Dyfrig Clo. CF6—3B 22
St Edeyrn's Clo. CF2—1H 11
St Edeyrn's Rd. CF2—1G 11
St Edwen Gdns. CF4—2C 10
St Fagan's Clo. CF5—5D 14
St Fagan's Ct. CF5—5D 14
St Fagan's Dri. CF5—1E 15
St Fagan's Rise. CF5—1G 15
St Fagan's Rd. CF5—2G 15
St Fagan's St. CF1—1D 20
St Francis Rd. CF4—2G 9
St George's Rd. CF4—4B 10
St Gilda's Rd. CF4—2D 10
St Gowan Av. CF4—2C 10
St Gwynno's Clo. CF6—2A 22
St Helen's Rd. CF4—3B 10

St Illtyd Clo. CF6—3B 22
St Ina Rd. CF4—2C 10
St Isan Rd. CF4—2C 10
St John's Cres. CF4—1G 9
St John's Cres. CF5—4F 17
St John's Pl. CF4—1G 9
St John's St. CF1—4A 18
(in two parts)
St Luke's Av. CF6—3E 23
St Lythan Clo. CF6—3A 22
St Malo Rd. CF4—1C 10
St Margaret's Clo. CF4—1G 9
St Margaret's Cres. CF2—1D 18
St Margaret's Pk. CF5—3A 16
St Margaret's Pl. CF4—1G 9
St Margaret's Rd. CF4—1G 9
St Mark's Av. CF4—4C 10
St Mark's Gdns. CF4—4C 10
St Mark's Rd. CF4—3E 23
St Martin's Clo. CF6—3E 23
St Martin's Cres. CF4—6D 4
St Mary's Rd. CF4—1G 9
St Mary St. CF1—4A 18
St Mellons Rd. CF3—4C 24
St Mellons Rd. CF4 & CF3—2G 5
to 3D 6
St Michael's Rd. CF5—2C 16
St Nicholas Clo. CF6—3A 22
St Paul's Av. CF6—3E 23
St Paul's Clo. CF6—3A 22
St Peter's Rd. CF6—3A 22
St Peter's St. CF2—2B 18
St Pierre Clo. CF3—3A 24
St Tanwg Rd. CF4—2C 10
St Teilo Clo. CF6—2B 22
St Teilos Ct. CF2—1D 18
St Winifred's Clo. CF6—3A 22
Salisbury Av. CF6—2F 23
Salisbury Clo. CF6—3F 23
Salisbury Rd. CF2—2B 18
Salop Pl. CF6—6E 21
Salop St. CF6—6E 21
Sanatorium Rd. CF1—4C 16
Sanctuary, The. CF5—6E 15
Sanderling Dri. CF3—6H 7
Sandon Rd. CF1—3B 18
Sandpiper Clo. CF3—5H 7
Sandringham Rd. CF2—6G 11
Santwell Ct. CF5—5B 20
Sanquhar St. CF2—4D 18
Sapphire St. CF2—2D 18
Saundersfoot Clo. CF5—6H 15
Saunders Rd. CF1—5A 18
School St. CF1—5B 18
Schooner Way. CF1—6B 18
Scott Ct. CF2—4F 11
Scott Rd. CF1—4A 18
Seaview Ct. CF6—1H 26
Seawall Rd. CF4—4F 19
Sedgemoor Rd. CF3—6E 7
Senghennydd Pl. CF2—2B 18
Senghennydd Rd. CF2—2A 18
Sevenoaks Rd. CF5—4F 15
Sevenoaks St. CF1—1D 20
Severn Ct. CF1—3F 17
Severn Gro. CF1—2F 17
Severn Rd. CF1—3F 17
Seymour St. CF2—3E 19
Shaftesbury Clo. CF4—2C 4
Shakespeare Av. CF6—1E 23
Shakespeare St. CF2—2C 18
Shamrock Rd. CF5—1G 15
Shaw Clo. CF3—6E 7
Shears Rd. CF5—2B 16
Shearwater Clo. CF6—6G 23
Sheerwater Clo. CF3—6G 7
Shelley Cres. CF6—1F 23
Shelley Wlk. CF2—2C 18
Sherborne Av. CF2—6G 5
Sheridan Clo. CF3—6D 6
Sherwood Ct. CF5—6D 8
Shirley Rd. CF2—5E 11
Silverstone Clo. CF3—5F 7
Silver St. CF2—3D 18
Singleton Rd. CF2—4E 19
Sir David's Clo. CF2—2D 16
Sir Ivor Pl. CF6—3B 22
Skaithmuir Rd. CF2—2F 19

Skelmuir Rd. CF2—2F 19
Sloper Rd. CF1—5F 17
Smeaton St. CF1—4G 17
Sneyd St. CF1—2F 17
Snipe St. CF2—2C 18
Snowden Rd. CF5—4F 15
Soberton Av. CF4—5D 10
Solva Av. CF4—5E 5
Somerset St. CF1—5G 17
Sophia Clo. CF1—3G 17
S. Clive St. CF1—2D 20
Southcourt Rd. CF3—5H 11
Southern Way. CF3—5B 12
Southey St. CF2—2C 18
(in two parts)
S. Luton Pl. CF2—4C 18
Southminster Rd. CF2—1D 18
S. Morgan Pl. CF1—4G 17
S. Park Rd. CF2—4F 19
South Rise. CF4—5E 5
South View. CF4—1B 2
S. View Dri. CF3—2E 13
Spencer's Row. CF5—6G 9
Spencer St. CF2—6A 11
Spinney Clo. CF5—3G 15
Spinney, The. CF4—3F 5
Splott Rd. CF2—3D 18
Springfield Gdns. CF4—5B 2
Springfield Pl. CF3—1F 17
Spring Gdns. Pl. CF2—2E 19
Spring Gdns. Ter. CF2—2E 19
Springhurst Clo. CF4—6F 3
Springwood. CF2—2H 11
Square, The. CF6—2A 22
Stacey Rd. CF2—2D 18
Stacey Rd. CF6—2A 22
Stadium Clo. CF1—5B 16
Stafford Rd. CF1—5G 17
Staines St. CF5—2D 16
Stallcourt Av. CF2—1D 18
Stanton Way. CF6—5G 23
Stanway Pl. CF5—4F 15
Stanway Rd. CF5—4F 15
Stanwell Cres. CF6—6F 21
Stanwell Rd. CF6—2F to 1G 23
Star St. CF2—3D 18
Station App. CF6—2G 23
Station Rd. CF4—4F 9
(Llandaff)
Station Rd. CF4—5D 4
(Llanishen)
Station Rd. CF4—2C 8
(Radyr)
Station Rd. CF6—2A 22
(Dinas Powis)
Station Rd. CF6—2G 23
(Penarth)
Station Ter. CF1—3B 18
Station Ter. CF3—3B 16
Station Ter. CF6—2G 23
Steep St. CF6—6E 21
Stenhousemuir Pl. CF2—2F 19
Stephen Newbury Clo. CF4
—3D 4
Stephenson St. CF1—4G 17
Stirling Rd. CF5—5E 15
Stockland St. CF1—1D 20
Stoneleigh Ct. CF1—2F 17
Stone Yd., The. CF1—4F 17
Storrar Rd. CF2—1G 19
Strathnairn St. CF2—1B 18
Stuart St. CF1—2F 21
Sturminster Rd. CF2—1E 19
Sudcroft St. CF1—5E 17
Sullivan Clo. CF3—6F 7
Sullivan Clo. CF6—4F 23
Sully Pl. CF6—2G 23
Sully Rd. CF6—6C to 1D 22
Sully Ter. CF6—2G 23
Sully Ter. La. CF6—3G 23
Summerau Ct. CF5—2E 17
Summerfield Av. CF4—5D 10
Summerfield Pl. CF4—2B 10
Summerhill Clo. CF3—4A 24
Summerland Clo. CF6—5B 20
Summerland Cres. CF6—5B 20
Sumner Clo. CF5—4E 9
Sundew Clo. CF5—5D 8

Sundew Clo. CF6—6C 20
Sunningdale Clo. CF2—3F 11
Sunnycroft Clo. CF6—3B 22
Sunnycroft La. CF6—3B 22
(in two parts)
Sun St. CF2—3D 18
Surrey St. CF5—3D 16
Sussex St. CF1—5H 17
Swallowhurst Clo. CF5—5D 14
Swanage Clo. CF3—4A 24
Swansea St. CF2—4E 19
Sweldon Clo. CF5—6F 15
Swift Clo. CF3—1D 12
Swinton St. CF2—3E 19
Sycamore Clo. CF6—3B 22
(Dinas Powis)
Sycamore Clo. CF6—5C 20
(Llandough)
Sycamore Pl. CF5—1H 15
Sycamore St. CF4—1A 2
Sycamore Tree Clo. CF4—1A 8
Sylvan Clo. CF5—6E 9
System St. CF2—3C 18

Tabor St. CF4—1A 2
Taff Embkmt. CF1—6H 17
Taffs Mead Embkmt. CF1
—5H 17
Taff St. CF1—4B 18
Taff St. CF4—4C 2
Taff Ter. CF4—2C 8
Tair Erw Rd. CF4—3B 10
Talbot St. CF1—3G 17
Talworth St. CF2—2C 18
Talybont Rd. CF5—4H 15
Tal-y-garn St. CF4—5D 10
Tanglewood Clo. CF4—3E 5
Tangmere Dri. CF5—5D 8
Tapley Clo. CF5—6G 15
Tarwick Dri. CF3—1E 13
Taunton Av. CF3—2E 13
Taunton Cres. CF3—2E 13
Tavistock St. CF2—2B 18
Taymuir Rd. CF2—1F 19
Teal St. CF2—2C 18
Teasel Av. CF6—6C 20
Tedder Clo. CF4—6D 4
Tegfan Clo. CF4—5C 4
Teifi Pl. CF5—4H 15
Teilo St. CF1—2F 17
Telford St. CF1—4G 17
Templeton Av. CF4—4B 4
Templeton Clo. CF4—4C 4
Tenby Clo. CF6—2C 22
Tennyson Rd. CF6—1E 23
Tensing Clo. CF4—4D 4
Tern Clo. CF3—5H 7
Terrence Perkins Clo. CF4—2D 4
Tewkesbury Pl. CF2—5E 11
Tewkesbury St. CF2—6A 11
Thackeray Cres. CF3—6D 6
Theobald Rd. CF5—4E 17
Theodora St. CF2—2E 19
Thesiger St. CF2—1A 18
Thistle Way. CF5—1C 16
Thomas St. CF1—6H 17
Thompson Av. CF5—2C 16
Thompson Pl. CF5—2C 16
Thorley Clo. CF3—2F 11
Thornbury Clo. CF4—1A 10
Thorn Gro. CF6—5G 23
Thornhill Rd. CF4—1A to 5B 4
Thornhill St. CF5—3E 17
Three Arches Av. CF4—1E 11
Thurston St. CF5—2C 16
Tidenham Rd. CF5—5H 15
Timbers Sq. CF2—1D 18
Tin St. CF2—3D 18
Tintagel Clo. CF4—3C 4
Tintern St. CF5—3E 17
Tiverton Dri. CF3—3C 12
Toftingall Av. CF4—2B 10
Tolgate Clo. CF1—2B 20
Ton-yr-ywen Av. CF4—2C 10
Topaz St. CF2—3D 18
Torrens Dri. CF2—3F 11

31

Torrington Rd. CF3—6E 7
Tower Hill. CF6—2H 23
Town Wall. CF1—4A 18
Towyn Rd. CF3—3E 13
Towy Rd. CF4—6E 5
Trade La. CF1—6A 18
Trade St. CF1—5A 18
Trafalgar Rd. CF2—1D 18
Trebanog Clo. CF3—1G 13
Trebanog Cres. CF3—2G 13
Treborth Rd. CF3—2G 13
Trecastle Av. CF4—4C 4
Trecynon Rd. CF3—2H 13
Tredegar St. CF1—4B 18
Tredelerch Rd. CF3—5C 12
Trefaser Cres. CF3—1G 13
Tregaron Rd. CF5—4F 15
Treharris St. CF2—2B 18
Treherbert St. CF2—1H 17
Trelai Ct. CF5—6G 15
Trelawney Av. CF3—4D 12
Trelawney Cres. CF3—4D 12
Tremadoc Wlk. CF3—2G 13
Trenchard Dri. CF4—6D 4
Trenewydd Rd. CF3—2G 13
Treorcky St. CF2—1A 18
Tresigin Rd. CF3—1G 13
Tresillian Ter. CF1—5A 18
Tresillian Way. CF1—5A 18
Trevethick St. CF1—4G 17
Trinity St. CF1—4A 18
Tristram Clo. CF4—3B 4
Troed y Rhiw. CF4—4G 3
Trowbridge Grn. CF3—1G 13
Trowbridge Rd. CF3—2F 13
Tudor Clo. CF5—2H 15
Tudor Clo. CF6—4G 23
Tudor La. CF1—5H 17
Tudors, The. CF3—6H 11
Tudor St. CF1—5H 17
Tulloch St. CF2—6G 11
Tummel Clo. CF2—2G 11
Turberville Pl. CF1—3F 17
Turner Rd. CF5—3D 16
Turnham Grn. CF3—5A 12
Turnpike CLo. CF6—1A 22
Tuscan Clo. CF6—6D 4
Tweedsmuir Rd. CF2—2F 19
Twyncyn. CF6—2A 22
Twyn-y-fedwen Rd. CF4—4B 10
Ty Bryncoch. CF1—4A 2
Ty-cefn Rd. CF5—3H 15
Ty Cerrig. CF2—5A 6
Ty-coch Rd. CF5—3G 15
Tydfil Pl. CF2—5F 11
Ty-draw Pl. CF2—6G 11
Ty-draw Rd. CF2—5F 11
Ty-Draw Rd. CF3—4H 5
Ty-fry Av. CF3—4D 12
Ty-fry Clo. CF3—3D 12
Ty-fry Gdns. CF3—3D 12
Ty-fry Rd. CF3—4D 12
Ty-glas Av. CF4—5C 4
Ty-glas Rd. CF4—6B 4
Ty Gwyn. CF2—4G 11
Ty-gwyn Av. CF2—5G 11
Ty-gwyn Cres. CF2—4G 11
Ty-gwyn Rd. CF2—4G 11
Ty-gwyn Rd. CF4—6A 4
Tyla. CF3—1A 24
Tyla Teg. CF4—5F 3
Tyler St. CF2—2E 19
Ty-mawr. CF3—5C 12

Ty-mawr Clo. CF3—5C 12
Ty-mawr Rd. CF3—5C 12
Ty-mawr Rd. CF4—2E to 4F 9
Tymynydd Clo. CF4—6B 2
Tynant. CF4—3H 9
Ty-nant Rd. CF4—4B 2
Ty-nant St. CF1—6G 17
Tyndall St. CF1—5B 18
Tyndall St. Industrial Area. CF1
—5B 18
Tyneside Rd. CF1—1H 21
Tynewydd. CF4—3G 9
Tynewydd Dri. CF3—1C 24
Ty'n-y-cae Gro. CF4—1A 10
Ty'n-y-coed La. CF2—6B 11
Ty'n-y-coed Pl. CF2—6B 11
Ty'n-y-parc Rd. CF4—2H 9
Ty'n-y-pwll Rd. CF4—2G 9
Ty parc Clo. CF5—5D 8
Ty-Rhiw. CF4—1B 2
Tyrhiw Est. CF4—1B 2
Tyrwhitt Cres. CF2—2E 11
Tyr Winch Rd. CF3—6F 7
Tyr-y-sarn Rd. CF3—4D 12
Ty-to-maen Clo. CF3—5G 7
Ty-wern Av. CF4—1A 10
Ty-wern Rd. CF4—1A 10

Ullswater Av. CF2—4E 11
Universal St. CF1—5H 17
University Pl. CF2—3E 19
Uphill Rd. CF3—2D 12
Uplands Cres. CF6—5C 20
Uplands Rd. CF3—5C 12
Uplands, The. CF4—1B 8
Uppercliff Clo. CF6—6G 21
Uppercliff Dri. CF6—1H 26
Up. Clifton St. CF2—2D 18
Up. Kincraig St. CF2—1C 18
Up. Meadow. CF5—6F 15
Uskley Ct. CF3—1G 13
Usk Rd. CF4—5E 5

Vachell Rd. CF5—4G 15
Vaindre Clo. CF3—3A 24
Vaindre Dri. CF3—3A 24
Vaindre La. CF3—3E 19
Vale Ct. CF6—2B 22
Vale Rd. CF2—2E 19
Vale View Clo. CF6—5B 20
Vale View Cres. CF6—5B 20
Van St. CF1—6G 17
Vaughan Av. CF5—1B 16
Velindre Pl. CF4—2F 9
Velindre Rd. CF4—2E 9
Vendre Clo. CF3—2A 24
Ventnor Pl. CF4—5B 10
Vere St. CF2—2C 18
Verlands Clo. CF5—1C 16
Victoria Av. CF5—3D 16
Victoria Av. CF6—2G 23
Victoria Pk. Rd. E. CF5—3D 16
Victoria Pk. Rd. W. CF5—3C 16
Victoria Pl. CF1—4A 18
Victoria Rd. CF4—2G 9
Victoria Rd. CF6—3F 23
Victoria Sq. CF6—2G 23
Vincent Rd. CF5—4A 16
Violet Pl. CF4—3B 10
Violet Row. CF2—1B 18
Virgil St. CF1—6G 17
Vishwell Rd. CF5—2D 16
Vista Rise. CF4—4D 5

Walford Pl. CF1—4F 17
Walker Rd. CF2—4E 19
Walk, The. CF2—3B 18
Walk, The. CF3—4C 12
Walnut Tree Clo. CF4—6A 2
Walpole Clo. CF3—5E 7
Wanderers Cres. CF5—5E 15
Warwick Pl. CF1—6H 17
Warwick St. CF1—6H 17
Wasdale Clo. CF2—5F 11
Washford Av. CF3—6E 7
Watchet Clo. CF3—2D 12
Waterhall Rd. CF5—6D 8
Waterloo Gdns. CF2—1D 18
Waterloo Rd. CF3 & CF2—5H 11
Waterston Rd. CF4—5H 9
Watford Rd. CF2—1F 19
Watson Rd. CF4—5G 9
Watton Clo. CF4—5C 4
Waunfach. CF2—6A 6
Waun-fawr Rd. CF4—1B 10
Waun-gron Rd. CF5—2B 16
Waun Lee Ct. CF2—5A 6
Wauntreoda Rd. CF4—3A 10
Waun-y-groes Av. CF4—6A 4
Waun-y-groes Rd. CF4—6A 4
Wavell Clo. CF4—1D 10
Waverley Clo. CF6—5C 20
Wedal Rd. CF4 & CF2—5E 11
Wedmore Rd. CF1—5G 17
Weekes Clo. CF4—6F 7
Welby Rd. CF5—4F 17
Wellfield Ct. CF3—3D 24
Wellfield Pl. CF2—1C 18
Wellfield Rd. CF2—1C 18
Wellfield Rd. CF3—3D 24
Wellington St. CF1—4F 17
Wellington St. CF4—4C 2
Wellright Rd. CF5—2H 15
Wells St. CF1—4F 17
Wellwood. CF3—4A 12
Well Wood Clo. CF5—5A 12
Well Wood Dri. CF6—3A 22
Welwyn Rd. CF4—2A 10
Wembley Rd. CF5—4E 17
Wanallt Ct. CF4—5H 3
Wenallt Rd. CF4—3G 3
Wentloog Clo. CF3—4D 12
Wentloog Rd. CF3—4D 12
Wentworth Clo. CF3—3A 24
Wentworth La. CF3—3A 24
Werfa St. CF2—6B 11
Wern Fawr La. CF3—5G 7
Wern-gethin La. CF3—2G &
1H 13
Wern Goch. CF2—1A 12
Wern-goch E. CF2—1G 11
Wern Goch W. CF2—1H 11
Wesley St. CF3—2E 13
Wesley Ct. CF6—2A 22
Wesley La. CF1—4B 18
Wessex St. CF5—3D 16
Westbourne Cres. CF4—3E 9
Westbourne Rd. CF4—3F 9
Westbourne Rd. CF4—4G 23
Westbury Ter. CF5—2D 16
W. Bute St. CF1—1G 21
W. Canal Wharf. CF1—5A 18
West Clo. CF1—1F 21
Western Av. CF5 & CF4—2B 16
to 4B 10
Western Dri. CF4—6A 10
Westfield Av. CF4—2A 10

Westfield Rd. CF4—3A 10
Westgate St. CF1—4H 17
West Gro. CF2—3B 18
West Lee. CF1—3G 17
W. Luton Pl. CF2—4C 18
Westminster Cres. CF2—6G 5
Westminster Dri. CF2—5G 5
Westmoreland St. CF5—4E 17
Weston Rd. CF3—2D 12
W. Orchard Cres. CF5—2C 16
West Rise. CF4—5E 5
West Rd. CF4—4F 9
West Ter. CF6—1G 23
West View. CF4—1B 2
Westville Rd. CF2—6G 11
Westville Wlk. CF2—6G 11
W. Wharf Rd. CF1—5A 18
(in two parts)
W. Wharf Rd. CF1—5C & 6C 18
(Butetown)
Wharfedale Rd. CF2—5B 6
Wharf Rd. E. CF1—5C 18
Wharf St. CF1—5B 18
Wharton St. CF1—4A 18
Wheatley Rd. CF5—4G 15
Whitaker Rd. CF2—1G 19
Whitchurch Pl. CF4—6A 11
Whitchurch Rd. CF4—4C 10
Whitcliffe Dri. CF6—5H 23
White Barn Rd. CF4—5B 4
Whitefield Rd. CF4—5G 9
Whitehall Av. CF3—4C 12
Whitehall Pde. CF3—4D 12
Whitehall Pl. CF3—4C 12
Whitehall Rd. CF5—6F 9
White Oaks Dri. CF3—5G 7
Whitesands Rd. CF4—4B 4
Whitland Clo. CF5—6D 8
Whitland Cres. CF5—6E 9
Whitmuir Rd. CF2—4E 19
Whittle Rd. CF1—6E 17
Widecombe Dri. CF3—4C 12
Wild Gdns Rd. CF2—2E 11
William St. CF1—2F 17
Williams Way. CF1—6A 18
Williton Rd. CF3—6E 7
Willowbrook Dri. CF3—6G 7 to
5A 24
Willow Clo. CF6—2E 23
Willow Ct. CF2—2C 18
Willowdale Clo. CF5—1G 15
Willowdale Rd. CF5—1F 15
Willowdene Way. CF3—3A 24
Willowmere. CF6—4B 20
Willows Av. CF2—3F 19
Willow Tree Clo. CF4—1A 8
Wilson Pl. CF5—5G 15
Wilson Rd. CF5—4F 15
Wilson St. CF2—2E 19
Winchester Av. CF3—5H 11
Windermere Av. CF2—3E 11
Windrush Pl. CF5—1H 15
Windsor Av. CF4—1B 8
Windsor Ct. CF2—3C 18
Windsor Ct. CF4—1B 8
Windsor Ct. CF6—2H 23
Windsor Cres. CF4—2C 8
Windsor Esplanade. CF1—2F 21
Windsor Grn. CF5—3A 16
Windsor Gro. CF4—1B 8
Windsor La. CF1—3B 18
Windsor La. CF6—6E 21
Windsor Pl. CF1—3B 18

Windsor Pl. CF6—1G 23
Windsor Rd. CF2—4C 18
Windsor Rd. CF4—2B 8
Windsor Rd. CF6—5C 20
Windsor Ter. CF1—2F 21
Windsor Ter. CF6—1H 26
Windsor Ter. La. CF6—1H 26
Windway Av. CF5—3C 16
Windway Rd. CF5—2B 16
Windy Ridge. CF6—3C 22
Wingate Dri. CF4—1D 10
Wingfield Rd. CF4—3F 9
Winnipeg Dri. CF2—3G 11
Withycombe Rd. CF3—6E 7
Witla Ct. Rd. CF3—2E 13
Wolfs Castle Av. CF4—4C 4
Womanby St. CF1—4A 18
Woodcock St. CF2—2C 18
Woodfield Av. CF4—3C 8
Woodland Cres. CF2—3G 11
Woodland Pl. CF6—1G 23
Woodland Rd. CF4—3F 9
Woodlands Pk. Dri. CF5—6G 15
Woodlands Pl. CF2—2C 18
Woodlands, The. CF4—3F 5
Woodlawn Way. CF4—2C 4
Woodside Ct. CF4—4E 5
Wood St. CF1—5A 18
Wood St. CF6—1G 23
Woodvale Av. CF2—6G 5
Woodville Rd. CF2—1A 18
Woolacombe Av. CF3—2E 13
Woolaston Av. CF2—2F 11
Woolmer Clo. CF5—5D 8
Worcester Ct. CF4—2F 11
Wordsworth Av. CF2—2C 18
Wordsworth Av. CF6—1E 23
Working St. CF1—4A 18
Worle Av. CF3—2D 12
Worle Pl. CF3—2D 12
Wrexham Ct. CF3—2G 13
Wroughton Pl. CF5—3A 16
Wyvenrne Rd. CF2—1A 18
Wyfan Pl. CF4—5B 10
Wyncliffe Rd. CF2—5C 6
Wyndham Arc. CF1—4A 18
Wyndham Cres. CF1—3F 17
Wyndham Pl. CF1—4G 17
Wyndham Rd. CF1—3F 17
Wyndham St. CF1—4G 17
Wyndham St. CF4—4C 2
Wyndham Ter. CF6—5E 5
Wyon Clo. CF5—4D 8

Yew St. CF4—1A 2
Yewtree Clo. CF5—1G 15
Y Goedwig. CF4—5G 3
Y Groes. CF4—6H 3
Yorath Rd. CF4—2H 9
York Pl. CF1—2D 20
York St. CF5—4E & 3E 17
Youldon Ho. CF6—2B 22
Ystrad Clo. CF4—4C 3
Ystrad St. CF1—1E 21

Zinc St. CF2—3D 18

Printed and bound in Great Britain by Halstan & Co. Ltd., Plantation Road, Amersham, Bucks.